The American Riddle Book

THE AMERICAN *Riddle* BOOK

By Carl Withers and Dr. Sula Benet
Illustrated by Marc Simont

Abelard-Schuman, New York

Copyright, 1954 by Carl Withers and Dr. Sula Benet
Library of Congress Catalog Card Number: 53-10845

SECOND PRINTING

Printed and bound in the United States of America
Published simultaneously in Canada by Nelson, Foster & Scott, Ltd.

A Word About This Book

THIS is called *The American Riddle Book* because it is designed to entertain young Americans. It contains well over a thousand items of the riddling sense and nonsense that have amused and entertained youngsters (and ofttimes their elders) in many countries, today and over the centuries. Every type of interesting riddle that the compilers could discover is represented.

Here are to be found hundreds of the *true riddles* which are in the great folklore tradition of the English speaking countries—and often of half the rest of the world besides. They are true riddles in the sense that they are meant to be guessed, and are reasonably guessable. That is, the solution always fits logically the terms of the question, no matter how artfully this has been constructed to lead the guesser astray. The art of riddling is the world's oldest quiz game, and in our grandparents' day it was a favorite pastime for adults. Still earlier, old legends tell us, it was a very serious sport indeed, for sometimes a kingdom or a life hinged on the solution of riddles. Succeeding generations of children still joyfully pit their wits against them.

Many of the true riddles are very beautiful in metaphor and language. (What flies forever and never rests?—The wind.) Many of the loveliest ones, in English as in other languages, are in rhyme, and sometimes these survive more for their charm as childhood jingles than because they are riddles. For example, all youngsters chant *Humpty Dumpty,* but few are ever asked to guess that he is an egg.

Like folktales, true riddles have traveled far and wide, from language to language and from continent to continent.

They often change their cultural dress along the way, yet riddles that are as old as Babylon leap from the lips of contemporary children.

Hundreds more of the riddles printed here are the clever or funny or merely absurd questions and answers that delight American children so much today. They are called riddles because they follow the true riddle's formal pattern in which a short provocative question is followed by a surprising answer. But they differ from the true riddle in that no listener is ever really expected, nor can reasonably be expected, to *guess* the answer. Most of them are *conundrums*, a type of riddle in which the solution generally depends upon a pun. (What animals go to bed with you?—Your calves.) Others have answers so anticlimactic or even so obvious that an intelligent child would hardly dare to offer them seriously as solutions. (Why does a rooster cross the road?—To get to the other side.) Riddles of this type have been called *teasing questions* or *verbal catches* or *sells*. In another type of question is only a "feeder" for an answering "punch line," and the whole resembles a joke or anecdote more than a true riddle. (What did one little inkdrop ask another little inkdrop?—Is your daddy in the pen too?) Yet the joke has been constrained, after a fashion, into the old riddle pattern. Whatever the sources of invention for this kind of word play, children love it dearly and embrace the products avidly into their folklore. The resulting pastime, of course, is far less a guessing game than one of taking in "victims" with catch questions, and it is often only a mode of displaying or exchanging verbal humor.

On the pages with named classifications appear alphabet riddles, arithmetical riddles, Bible riddles, bird riddles and many other special categories that have interested riddlers, riddle gatherers and even riddle inventors over the years. These range from the rather macabre neck riddles of hoary antiquity to the most up-to-date riddling nonsense clustering about the popular numskull character, Little Moron. It was felt that more emphasis would be given to the variety of the riddling art by grouping these materials together than by scattering them through the general pages.

The art of riddling runs round the world, and a special feature of *The American Riddle Book* is the hundred or so riddles included from the folklore of as many other nations, local regions and tribal groups. They are offered as a contrast with those more familiar to us, and as a kind of token tribute to the wealth of riddles—amusing, beautiful and often exotic —to be found in cultures other than our own. They were gathered from printed collections in many languages and from friends. In adapting English versions of foreign riddles, as well as in translating from another language to English, the compilers have felt free to simplify riddles when necessary to render them more easily understandable. They have also felt free to turn a non-interrogative riddle into a question or to add to it some such querying catch phrase as "What is it?" or "Who am I?" They have always tried, however, to adhere rather strictly to the intellectual content of the original riddle, that is, to omit no detail of the problem posed for solution. There is, of course, much loss in a riddle's beauty through translating it from rhyme to prose or through other factors of lost rhythm and association. It is intended to follow the present book shortly with another that will give full representation to the riddles of other lands, with appropriate bibliography and commentary. Riddles still have many varied and remarkable functions in the world.

The English language riddles that fill most of the space in this book came from many sources. Some were gathered directly by the senior compiler through fieldwork with children in New York City and in several American rural communities. Others came from youthful and older friends who were asked to remember what riddles they had heard recently or could recollect from childhood. Many came from a research project in children's folklore carried on during a number of years through short field research assignments undertaken by college freshmen. Many came from printed sources ranging from regional collections in professional folklore journals to the great variety of popular riddle and conundrum books, published over many years, that are accessible in the New York Public Library.

A list of all the publications consulted in selecting the English and foreign riddles would run to many pages, and it has been decided to forego it in the present book. Special help and stimulation came from the publications of the following American scholars: R. S. Boggs, Paul G. Brewster, A. H. Fauset, Herbert Halpert, H. M. Hyatt, Elsie Clews Parsons, A. E. Perkins, Vance Randolph, Stith Thompson, and Archer Taylor. Professor Taylor's book, *English Riddles from Oral Tradition* (University of California Press, 1951), is the definitive comparative study of riddles in English. Its excellent bibliography lists many of the relevant works of all the other scholars listed above (except Professor Stith Thompson's *The Folktale*), as well as most of the collections consulted in gathering the foreign riddles.

Thanks are also due to Mr. William J. Gedney and Mr. Chit Phumsak of Bangkok, Thailand, for sending a collection of thirty-seven Thai riddles; to Mr. Anthony Leeds of New York City for a collection of riddles from Brazil; to Mr. William Mangin of New Haven, Connecticut, for a collection of Peruvian riddles; and to Professor David McAllester of Middletown, Connecticut, for a collection of Comanche Indian riddles. One riddle from each collection is included here.

*When first I appear I seem mysterious,
But when I'm explained I'm nothing serious.*
—A riddle.

What goes forever and never stops?
—*The wind.*

What do you have that is easiest to part with?
—*Your comb.*

What has eighteen legs and catches flies?
—*A baseball team.*

Why is a lollipop like a race horse?
—*The more you lick it the faster it goes.*

Why are acrobats so strong?
—*Because they live on ropes and poles.*

What goes all over the house but **touches** nothing in the house?
—*Your voice.*

Thirty-two white horses on a red hill,
Now they stamp, now they champ,
Now they stand still.
—Teeth.

Why is it bad to look at Niagara Falls too long?
—*You might get a cataract in your eye.*

What is it that you should never give without keeping it yourself?
—*Your word.*

Why is an elephant an unwelcome guest?
—*Because he has to bring his trunk along.*

Why are ghosts like writing pads?
—*Because they appear in sheets.*

What has seven legs and no head and wags its tail?
—*A dog with his head jammed into a three-legged pot.*

What word can you pronounce quicker by adding a syllable to it?
—*Quick.*

*Though I dance at a ball,
I am nothing at all.
What am I?*

—A shadow.

What animal changes his size twice daily?

—*The watchdog. You let him out every
night and take him in every morning.*

Why did Johnny take a ruler to bed?

—*To see how long he slept.*

What has a horn and is dangerous to walk
in front of?

—*An automobile.*

What is the best way to raise strawberries?

—*With a spoon.*

What goes up into the air white and comes
down yellow and white?

—*An egg tossed into the air.*

CHAIN RIDDLES*

Beyond the seas there is an oak,
And in that oak there is a nest,
And in that nest there is an egg,
And in that egg there is a yolk
Which calls together Christian folk.

    —A church, the steeple, the bell and the clapper.

There was a little green house:
And inside the little green house
There was a little brown house;
And inside the little brown house
There was a little yellow house;
And inside the little yellow house
There was a little white house;
And inside the little white house
There was a little sweet heart.

    —A walnut.

On yonder hill there is a mill:
Around that mill there is a walk;
Under the walk there is a key.
What is the name of this mill?

    —Milwaukee.

On the hill there is a house,
And in that house there is a room,
And in that room there is a closet,
And in that closet there is a coat,
And in that coat there is a pocket,
And in that pocket there is a little buffalo's head.

    —A buffalo nickel.

---
* The terms "chain riddle" and "neck riddle" (p. 108) were invented by Professor Archer Taylor.

*A riddle! a riddle!
A hole in the middle.*
    —A doughnut.

What holds the moon up?
—*The moon beams.*

When is a boy most deeply immersed in his business? —*When he goes swimming.*

What fruit do we get from the electric plant? —*Currents.*

How many boiled eggs can a giant eat on an empty stomach?

—*Only one—after that his stomach isn't empty.*

Can a black dog change color in the moonlight?

—*Yes, he sometimes turns to bay.*

What can speak every language in the world? —*An echo.*

*Up and down, up and down,
Touches neither sky nor ground.*

—A pump handle.

Why did the kangaroo mother scold her children?
—*For eating crackers in bed.*

How do little fish make their living?
—*They start out on a very small scale.*

What goes up every time the rain comes down?
—*Umbrellas.*

What is the difference between an old dime and a new nickel?
—*Five cents.*

What is the difference between a prize fighter and a man with a cold?
—*One knows his blows and the other blows his nose.*

Do hens ever become roosters?
—*Yes, they become roosters every night when they fly up on the chicken roost.*

What runs around town all day, and lies under the bed at night with its tongue hanging out?
—*Your shoe.*

*There was a man who had no eyes,
Who walked abroad to see the skies.
He saw a tree with apples on;
He picked no apples off—he left no apples on.*

—A one-eyed man saw a tree with only two apples on it. He picked one and left one.

Which side of an apple is the left side?

—*The side you haven't eaten.*

How do we know that ants are very sociable?

—*Because they go to every picnic.*

Why do policemen wear blue suspenders?

—*To hold their pants up.*

What is the difference between a pretty girl and a mouse?

—*One charms the he's and the other harms the cheese.*

What runs everywhere and leaves just one track?

—*A wheelbarrow.*

BARNYARD ANIMALS

What pig is a very small man?—*A* PIG*my*.

What dog lives in the sky?—*The* DOG*star*.

What cow has no courage—*A* COW*ard*.

What goat adorns a chin?—*A* GOAT*ee*.

What cat can throw a heavy weight?—*A* CAT*apult*.

What bull is often shot?—*A* BULL*et*.

What sheep is very shy?—SHEEP*ish*.

What boar pays for his dinner?—*A* BOAR*der*.

What ox do you breathe?—OX*ygen*.

What cock must stay out of the kitchen?—*A* COCK*roach*.

What pup is moved with a string?—*A* PUP*pet*.

What ram is very strong?—*A* RAM*part*.

What horse lives underground?—*A* HORSE*radish*.

What goose is very sour? —*A* GOOSE*berry*.

Comes in at every window,
And every door crack.
Runs round and round the house,
And never leaves a track.
—The wind.

When are cooks most ferocious?
—*When they beat eggs and whip cream.*

What is the difference between an elephant and a flea?
—*An elephant can have fleas, but a flea can't have elephants.*

Three large ladies went walking under one umbrella. Why didn't they get wet?
—*It wasn't raining.*

Do mountains have ears?
—*Yes, they have mountaineers.*

What can a whole apple do that a half apple can't?
—*It can look round.*

Black within and red without,
Four corners roundabout.

—A chimney.

Why do goldfish always seem so well traveled?

—Because they've all been around the globe.

Why is your nose in the middle of your face?

—Because it's the (s)center.

With which hand should you stir your cocoa?

—With either, but it's better to stir it with a spoon.

Why is a prudent man like a pin?

—His head keeps him from going too far.

What is the largest jewel in the world?
—A baseball diamond.

What runs over the floor in the daytime and stands in the corner at night.

—A broom.

*Thomas A. Tattamus took two T's
To tie two tups to two tall trees,
To frighten the terrible Thomas A. Tattamus!
Tell me: how many T's there are in that?*
                                    —Two.

Why are hot rolls like caterpillars?
—*Because they make the butterfly.*

I saw a duck swimming in a pond and a dog sitting on its tail. Wasn't that odd?
—*No. The dog was sitting on its own tail.*

When are your eyes not eyes?
—*When the wind makes them water.*

What happens to a deer when an Indian shoots at him and misses?
—*He has an arrow escape.*

Why is a cloud like Santa Claus?
—*Because it holds the rain, dear (reindeer)!*

Why do white sheep eat so much more than black sheep?
—*Because there are so many more of them.*

ALPHABET RIDDLES

What letter is a large body of water?
—C (*sea*).

What letter can fly? —J (*jay*).

What letter is a busy insect? —B (*bee*).

What letter can read? —I (*eye*).

What letter grows in the garden?
—P (*pea*).

What letter is used in a billiard game?
—Q (*cue*).

What letter do people drink? —T (*tea*).

What letter is part of a house?
—L (*ell*).

What letter grazes in the pastures?
—U (*ewe*).

What letter is an exclamation?
—O, or G.

DOUBLE LETTERS

What two letters creep up a wall?—I V (*ivy*).

What two letters describe a slippery sidewalk?—I C.

What girls' names can you spell with two letters?
    L C or K T or L N.

What do old apples do?—D K.

What must the winner of a game do?—X L.

Can you spell annoy with only one letter?—TT (*tease*).

As I went through the garden gap,
Whom should I meet but Dick Redcap?
He had a stick in his hand and a stone in his throat—
Answer this riddle and I'll give you my goat.
— A cherry on a tree.

Why is a dog chasing a rabbit like a bald-headed man?
—*He makes a little hare (hair) go a long way.*

Why is a crow on a limb like a penny?
—*Because the head is on one side and the tail on the other.*

How can you always find a liar out?
—*Go to his house when he isn't in.*

What always remains down, even when it flies up in the air?
—*A feather.*

What often strikes you in the face, yet you can never see it?
—*The wind.*

Rough on the outside, smooth within,
Nothing can enter but a sharp flat thing.
When it enters it wiggles about,
And that is when the goodie comes out.
                              —An oyster.

Why is a baby like a wheatfield?

—*First he's cradled, then he's threshed and later he becomes the flour (flower) of the family.*

What would tickle a fat man a great deal?

—*A fly on his nose.*

What would be more trouble than a giraffe with a sore throat?

—*A centipede with a corn on each foot.*

How are farmers cruel to their corn?

—*They always pull its ears.*

What is the most important use for cowhide?

—*It holds the cow together.*

What do you break by naming it?

—*Silence.*

Four posts up and four posts down;
Soft in the middle but hard all around.

—A bed.

Whom do the mermaids smile at?
—*All the swells of the ocean.*

How do the mermaids tie up their hair?
—*With a marine band.*

What does the steamer Queen Mary weigh just before leaving New York harbor?
—*She weighs anchor.*

When is a castle like a fish?
—*When it is scaled.*

Would it offend a sparrow to call him a quail?
—*Yes. You would be making game of him.*

What has a tongue but can't eat?
—*A wagon.*

LITTLE MORON RIDDLES

Why did the moron drive his car off the cliff?
—*He wanted to try out his new air brakes.*

Why did the moron sleep on the chandelier?
—*Because he was a light sleeper.*

Why did the moron lock his father in the icebox?
—*Because he likes cold pop.*

Why did the moron sit on top of the house?
—*He had heard that the treats were on the house.*

Why did the moron cut his finger off?
—*Because he wanted to write shorthand.*

Why did the moron throw all his nails away?
—*Because their heads were on the wrong end.*

Why did the moron eat dynamite?
—*He wanted his hair to grow out in bangs.*

Why did the moron throw his clock out the window?
—*He liked to see time fly.*

Why was the moron able to buy ice at half-price?
—*Because it was melted.*

Why did the moron always walk tiptoe past the medicine cabinet?
—*He didn't want to wake up the sleeping pills.*

Why did the moron go into the street with his bread and butter?
—*He was looking for the traffic jam.*

Did he find it?
—*Yes, a truck came along and gave him a big jar.*

Why did the moron take his nose apart?
—*He wanted to see what made it run.*

What did the moron do when he thought he was dying?
—*He moved to the living room.*

Two legs sat on three legs,
Chewing on one leg.
In came four legs,
Snatched up one leg,
And ran away.
Up jumped two legs
And threw three legs
After four legs,
To make four legs
Bring one leg back!

—A man sat on a stool, eating a chicken leg. His dog snatched the chicken leg and ran away. The man threw the stool at the dog.

What do hippopotamuses have that no other animal has?
—*Little hippopotamuses.*

What kind of broadcaster is like a vegetable you eat daily?
—*A commentator (a common 'tater).*

Why is a good boxer like grandfather's clock?
—*Neither works long without striking.*

Why does a chair with a broken leg dislike you? —*It can't bear you.*

Jack lives on one side,
Tom on the other,
Yet neither one
Can see his brother.

—Ears.

How do we know that bears like beer?
—*Because they're always bruin (brewin').*

Why is a big snowstorm a very good joke?
—*Because everybody sees the drift.*

Why should no one ever court a girl in a garden?

—*Because the corn has ears, the potatoes have eyes, and the beans talk (beanstalk).*

How did the garden laugh at the gardener?

—*It said, "hoe, hoe!"*

Why is a boy turning a somersault no longer a boy?

—*Because he is turning turtle.*

What word contains all twenty-six letters?
—*Alphabet.*

BIRDS RIDDLES

What bird is easiest to deceive?—*A gull.*

What bird can lift the heaviest weight?—*The crane.*

What bird is very religious?—*A cardinal.*

What bird should fly the fastest?—*The swift.*

What bird reminds you of a good time?—*A lark.*

What is the craziest bird?—*A loon.*

What is the most foolish bird?—*A little goose.*

What bird should shrink from danger?—*The quail.*

What bird always goes to the table with you?—*Your swallow.*

What birds remind you of an engaged couple?—*Lovebirds.*

What is the greediest bird?—*The gobbler.*

What is the hardest bird to read about in fairy tales?
—*The roc (rock).*

How do we know that one bird is insane?
—*Because he's always a raven (a-ravin').*

*As I was going down the lane,
I met a man who was doing the same:
He tipped his hat an' drew his cane,
And in this riddle I've told you his name.*

—Andrew.

Why do giraffes eat so very little?

—*Because they must make a little go a very long way.*

For what man must you always remove your hat?

—*For the barber.*

What are the finest animals on earth?

—*Ground mice.*

Why did the city rat gnaw a hole in the floor?

—*He wanted to see the floor show.*

What is the difference between a falling star and a heavy fog?

—*One is missed from heaven and the other is mist from earth.*

What roof is always wet?

—*The roof of your mouth.*

*Old Mother Twitchett, she had but one eye,
And a great long tail that she let fly;
And every time she went through a gap,
She left a bit of her tail in the trap.*

—*A needle and thread.*

How do we know that mosquitos are very happy?

—*Because they always sing at their work.*

What goes all the way from New York to San Francisco without moving an inch?

—*The highway.*

Why could nobody play cards on the Ark?

—*Because Noah sat on the deck.*

What has eight legs and can sing very loud?

—*A male quartet.*

Why do people always put their right shoe on first?

—*It would be foolish to put the wrong shoe on first.*

What belongs to you that your friends use oftener than you do?

—*Your name.*

*Railroad crossing! Look out for the cars!
Can you spell that without any "r's"?*

—T, H, A, T.

Why are chickens such big eaters?
—*Because they eat a peck at a time.*

What birds have wings yet cannot fly?
—*Dead birds.*

Why do Eskimos always have fresh air to breathe?
—*Because it is kept on ice.*

What is the difference between a man and a banana peel?

—*A man often throws a banana peel in the gutter, and a banana peel sometimes throws a man in the gutter.*

Why do lazy boys have to go to school?
—*The school won't come to them.*

What does not exist yet has a name?
—*Nothing.*

*Brothers and sisters have I none,
But that man's father is my father's son.*

—*A man is speaking of his own son.*

How many legs has a mule if you call its tail a leg?

—*Only four. Calling its tail a leg doesn't make it one.*

What is the difference between a coat and a baby?

—*You wear a coat and you were a baby.*

What do people do in a watch factory?

—*They just stand around and make faces.*

Who is the smallest man in history?

—*The sailor who fell asleep on his watch.*

What can run faster uphill than downhill?—*Fire.*

KINSHIP RIDDLES

Two people sat down on a log to rest. One was the father of the other but the other was not his son. What kin were they?

—*A father and a daughter.*

Two fathers and two sons went duck hunting. Each shot a duck but they shot only three ducks in all. How could this be?—*The hunters were a man, his son and his grandson.*

A beggar's brother died but the man who died had no brother. How could that be?—*The beggar was a woman.*

If Tom's father is Bob's son, what kin is Bob to Tom?

—*Tom's grandfather.*

What kin is the door to the doormat?—*It's just a step fa'ther!*

If Mary falls off a fence, why can't her brother Jerry help her up?—*How could he be a brother and assist 'er too?*

Which of your kin is nearest you at the table?

—*Your nap-kin.*

Crooked as a snake, flat as a plate,
Ten thousand horses couldn't pull it straight.

—A river.

What did the mother possum say when she couldn't find her little possums?

—*Oh dear, I've had my pocket picked!*

Why shouldn't you gossip in the wheat-field?

—*You might shock the wheat.*

Why are people so tired on April 1?

—*They've all just finished a March of thirty-one days.*

How did the Dark Ages get their name?

—*It was Knight time when they occurred.*

What runs over the pasture all day, and sits in the cupboard all night?

—*Milk.*

Yonder on the hill
Stands a big red bull;
He eats and he eats,
But he never gets full.
—A threshing machine.

Why should we feel sorry for sheep?
—*Because they get fleeced so often.*

What suits last longer than people want them to?
—*Lawsuits.*

Why is New York City like a flashlight?
—*It has a Battery.*

Why is a dog dressed more warmly in summer than in winter?
—*In winter he wears only a fur coat, but in summer he wears that same coat and pants.*

What is it that is very black yet enlightens the whole world?
—*Ink.*

I'm in everyone's way,
Yet no one I stop;
My four arms every day in every way play,
And my head is nailed on at the top.
—A turnstile.

Why are a rooster's feathers always smooth?
—*Because he carries a fine comb.*

Why do people put stakes by a tomato plant?
—*To make the tomato "ketch up."*

What has more feet in winter than in summer?
—*A skating pond.*

What is the difference between a beautiful dancer and a duck?
—*The dancer goes quick on her legs and the duck goes quack on her legs.*

Why is your eye like a boy being whipped?
—*Because it's under the lash.*

What has four legs and flies?
—*A horse in the summertime.*

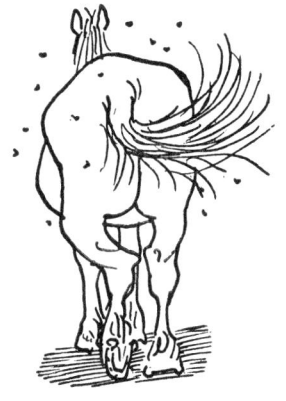

WORD CHARADES

My first makes company,
My second shuns company,
My third gathers a company,
My whole puzzles a company.
What am I?

—*A co-nun-drum.*

My first is a reflection,
My second is not so much,
My whole is none at all.

—*Thought-less.*

My first I hope you are,
My second I see you are,
My whole I know you are.

—*Wel-come.*

My first is everywhere,
My second is very flat,
My whole flies very fast.

—*Air-plane.*

My first is a pronoun,
My second is used at weddings,
My whole lives in the sea.

—*Her-ring.*

My first drives a horse,
My second is needy,
My third is a nickname,
My whole is a bird.

—*Whip-poor-will.*

My first is a dirty animal,
My second is at the end of it,
My whole is what little girls wear to school.

—*Pig-tail.*

*Who may marry many a wife
And yet stay single all his life?*
—A clergyman.

When does a caterpillar improve in behavior?
—*When it turns over a new leaf.*

If you were a carpenter helping to build a mushroom city, what kind of tools should you use?
—*Toadstools (toad's tools).*

What smells the best in every bakery?
—*The nose.*

Why shouldn't you laugh at a fat man?
—*You should never laugh at anybody else's expanse.*

Why is a nutmeg like the window of a jail?
—*It has to be grated to be useful.*

What has hands but never washes its face?
—*A clock.*

*Crooked as a rainbow,
Has teeth like a cat.
Guess all your lifetime—
You can't guess that!*

—A saw.

What did the backwoods cat tell her kittens about the world?

—*It's* FUR *from one end to the other.*

What do you see on every hand when you go out on a cold morning?
—*Gloves.*

If a boy found a dollar in every pocket of his pants, what would he probably have?

—*Somebody else's pants on.*

How can you tell a hill from a pill?
—*You can go up a hill, but a pill goes down you.*

*As I went up the heeple steeple,
There I met a heap of people.
Some were nick and some were nack;
Some were the color of an old brown sack.*
—Ants.

A frog, a duck and a skunk went to town to see the circus, but did they all get in?

—*The frog did because he had a greenback and the duck did because he had a bill, but they wouldn't let the skunk in because he had only a (s)cent and it was bad.*

Why was Washington buried at Mount Vernon?

—*Because he was dead.*

Why is a hat like a king?
—*Because it has a crown.*

What can stay alive only in fire?
—*A live coal.*

What is always before you yet you can never see it?
—*Your future.*

FAMOUS PROBLEMS

A duck behind two ducks,
A duck before two ducks,
A duck in the middle.
How many ducks in all?

—Three.

FROG IN THE WELL

A frog fell into a well twelve feet deep. He could jump three feet, but every time he jumped three feet he fell back two feet. How many times did he have to jump to get out of the well?

—*The tenth jump took him out.*

THE FOX, THE GOOSE AND THE CORN

A man started to town with a fox, a goose and a sack of corn and came to a stream which he had to cross in a boat. He could take only one across at a time, and he could not leave the fox alone with the goose or the goose alone with the corn. How did he get them all safely over?

—*He took the goose over first and came back. Then he took the fox across and brought the goose back. Next he took the corn over. He came back alone and took the goose over.*

My face is marked,
My hands keep moving;
I've no time to play—
I must run all day.
                    —A clock.

Why is a horse so cheap to feed?
—Because he eats best when he hasn't a bit in his mouth.

Why is a star like an old barn?
—Both contain R, A, T, S.

Why is a baby like a nation at war?
—Because it is in arms.

At which end of a street car is it best to get off?
—It makes little difference, since both ends stop.

A man came home late without his key and found all the doors and windows of his house locked. How did he get in?
—He walked round and round the house until he was all in.

What gets wetter and wetter the more it dries?
—A towel.

· 41 ·

*What's in the church
But not the steeple?
The parson has it,
But not the people.*

   —The letter R.

What is the best way to keep fish from smelling?

—*Cut off their noses.*

Why should you always carry a watch when crossing a desert?

—*Because there's a spring in it.*

Who earns his living without ever doing a day's work?

—*A night watchman.*

What is the difference between an oak tree and a tight shoe?

—*The oak makes acorns and the tight shoe makes corns ache.*

Why is a mouse like hay?

—*Because the cat'll (cattle) eat it.*

What is round as the moon and black as coal?

—*A frying pan.*

He wears a hat stuck on his neck
Because he has no head;
And many a time his hat comes off
When we are sick and old:
　　　　　—A bottle of medicine.

Which is bigger, Mrs. Bigger or Mrs. Bigger's baby?
—*The baby is just a little Bigger.*

Two boys went hunting and shot a jaybird, which they roasted and ate. What was their telephone number?
—281J (*Two ate one jay*).

When does a dentist appear grouchy?
—*When he is looking down in the mouth.*

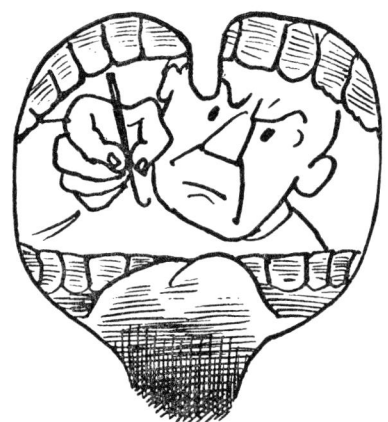

What do the neighbors of a horn player do that his fingers do?
—*They move quickly.*

What is better than presence of mind in an automobile accident?
—*Absence of body.*

What has a hundred legs but can't walk?
—*Fifty pairs of pants.*

WHAT'S IN A WORD?

What are the biggest ants in the world?—G*i*ANTS.

If you planted a puppy, what tree would come up?
—A DOG*wood.*

What pins taste best in soup?—*Terra*PINS.

What two beaux does a girl take everywhere?—*Her el*BOWS.

What bus found room for the most people?—*Colum*BUS.

At what age should people marry?—*At a parson*AGE.

What driver never gets arrested?—*A screw*DRIVER.

What pets make the loudest music?—*Trum*PETS.

On what kind of vines does beef grow?—*On bo*VINES.

What motive did the inventor of steam engines have in mind?—*A loco*MOTIVE.

What is the ugliest hood in the world?—*A false*HOOD.

Why is a baby boy always welcome?
—*Because he never comes a*MISS.

What cat do you always find in a library?—*A* CAT*alogue.*

What pine has the sharpest needles? —*The porcu*PINE.

Riddle come, riddle come ruckup!
What fell down and stuck up?
—A fork.

Why is a hot roll like a butterfly before it becomes a butterfly?

—*A hot roll is the grub that makes the butterfly.*

Why are chickens' necks like doorbells on Sunday?

—*Because that's the day they are most often wrung (rung) for company.*

When does a man become chicken-hearted?

—*When he is henpecked.*

What bow can nobody tie or untie?
—*A rainbow.*

Is it safe to write a letter on an empty stomach?

—*Perhaps. But it's better to write it on paper.*

What is the smallest bridge in the world?
—*The bridge of your nose.*

*Daffy-down-dilly has come to town,
In a yellow petticoat and a green gown.*
                        —A dandelion.

How can a boy have four hands?
—*By doubling his fists.*

When is a teapot like a puppy?
—*When your tea's in it (you're teasin' it).*

What did old King Neptune say when the seas dried up?
—*I haven't an ocean (a notion)!*

What is the difference between a farmer sowing and a woman sewing?
—*He will gather what he sows and she will sew what she gathers.*

A nickel and a dime were crossing a bridge and the nickel fell off. Why didn't the dime fall too?
—*He had more sense (cents) than the nickel.*

What do you lose every time you stand up?
—*Your lap.*

What has a trunk, but needs no key;
Has a big bark, but won't bite me?
—A tree.

What very fastidious animal reminds you of a flower?
—*A dandy lion (dandelion).*

What is it that, though blind itself, can guide the blind?
—*A walking stick.*

If a boy swallowed firecrackers, when would you know he was all right?
—*After hearing the last report.*

What's the difference between a boy without a nickel and a pillow?
—*The boy is hard up and the pillow is soft down.*

CATCH PROBLEMS

EARS IN A STUMP

A squirrel finds six ears of corn in a hollow stump. How many trips must the squirrel make to take the corn away, if he can carry only three ears out of the stump at each trip?

—*Six, because he has to carry his own ears out each time.*

THE PEACOCK

If you owned a peacock that laid eggs in your neighbor's yard, who would own the eggs?

—*Peacocks don't lay eggs.*

COWS IN THE CORNFIELD

A man's two cows disappeared and he found them together in his cornfield. One was facing north and the other was facing south, yet they could see each other. How?

—*They were facing each other.*

FOOD AND WATER

A man was locked up for a month in a room that had nothing in it but a bed and a calendar, and nobody brought him anything to eat or drink. How did he live?

—*He drank from the spring in the bed and ate dates off the calendar.*

THE RUNAWAY BALLOON

If a man and a goose were in a runaway balloon and the man had no parachute, how could he get down?

—*He could pluck the goose.*

GRAMMAR

Is it better to say, "The yolk of an egg *is* white," or "The yolk of an egg *are* white"?

—*Neither is right. An egg yolk is yellow.*

*As I was going to St. Ives,
I met a man with seven wives.
Each wife had seven sacks,
Each sack had seven cats,
Each cat had seven kits.
Kits, cats, sacks, and wives,
How many were going to St. Ives?*
—One.

Why do camels always appear pugnacious?
—*Because they have their backs up.*

What color is most easily heard?
—*A loud color.*

Why is a boat full of water like a man in jail? —*Because it needs bailing out.*

When should you really kick about a nice Christmas present? —*When it's a football.*

How would you punctuate, "I saw a dollar bill on the sidewalk"?
—*Just make a dash after it.*

*Opens like a barn door,
Shuts up like a bat.
I'll bet you a dollar
You can't guess that.*

— Umbrella.

Why is a cat climbing over a high fence like a high hill?

—*Because it's a-mountin'.*

Can you prove that a cat has three tails?

—*Yes: No cat has two tails. One cat has one tail more than no cat. Therefore, one cat has three tails.*

Why is a room packed with married people like an empty room?

—*Because there's not a single person in it.*

If Bob has a whole apple and Tom has only a bite, what should Tom do?

—*Scratch it.*

What's the difference between a motorman and a bad cold?

—*One knows the stops and the other stops the nose.*

What is full of holes and yet holds water?

—*A sponge.*

*Little Nancy Etticoat
Wears a white petticoat
And a red nose;
The longer she stands,
The shorter she grows.*
—A candle.

What little animal would you like to be on a cold day?
—*A little 'otter.*

On what day of the year do children talk the least?
—*On the shortest day.*

Which is better, an old five-dollar bill or a new one?
—*Any old five-dollar bill is better than a new one.*

When did the pine tree pine?
—*When it saw the weeping willow.*

What goes all over town from door to door, and never enters any door?
—*The sidewalk.*

TREES
What tree is very grouchy?—*The crab.*
What tree can fly through the air?—*The locust.*
What tree acts most sadly?—*The pine.*
What tree do you wear in bad weather? —*The rubber tree.*
What tree sounds most like you?—*The yew.*
What tree grows in your hand?—*A palm.*
What trees can burn up without changing their name?
 —*Ashes.*

What tree can you put in a bottle?—*A cork.*
What tree is older than other trees?—*The elder.*

Has a big mouth and never speaks;
Has a soft bed and never sleeps.

—A river.

Why do Eskimos weep so much?

—*Because every Eskimo must have his daily blubber.*

If a bear entered a drygoods store, what would he want?

—*He would want muslin (muzzlin').*

Who is always happiest when he finds everything very dull?

—*A scissors grinder.*

What kind of oats are generally sown at night?

—*Wild oats.*

If you saw a counterfeit dime lying in the street, should you leave it or pick it up?

—*Pick it up. You might get arrested for passing it.*

What has a foot and a head but can't walk or think?

—*A hill.*

I have a little sister —
They call her Peep, Peep.
She wades in the water,
Deep, deep, deep.

She climbs up the mountain,
High, high, high.
My poor little sister,
She has but one eye.
—*A star.*

Why should we all pity turtles?
—*Because theirs is a hard case.*

Who always walks behind a star?
—*A policeman.*

When do you see acrobats in a dining room?
—*When there are tumblers on the table.*

Why is a quarrel like a bargain?
—*Because it takes two to make one.*

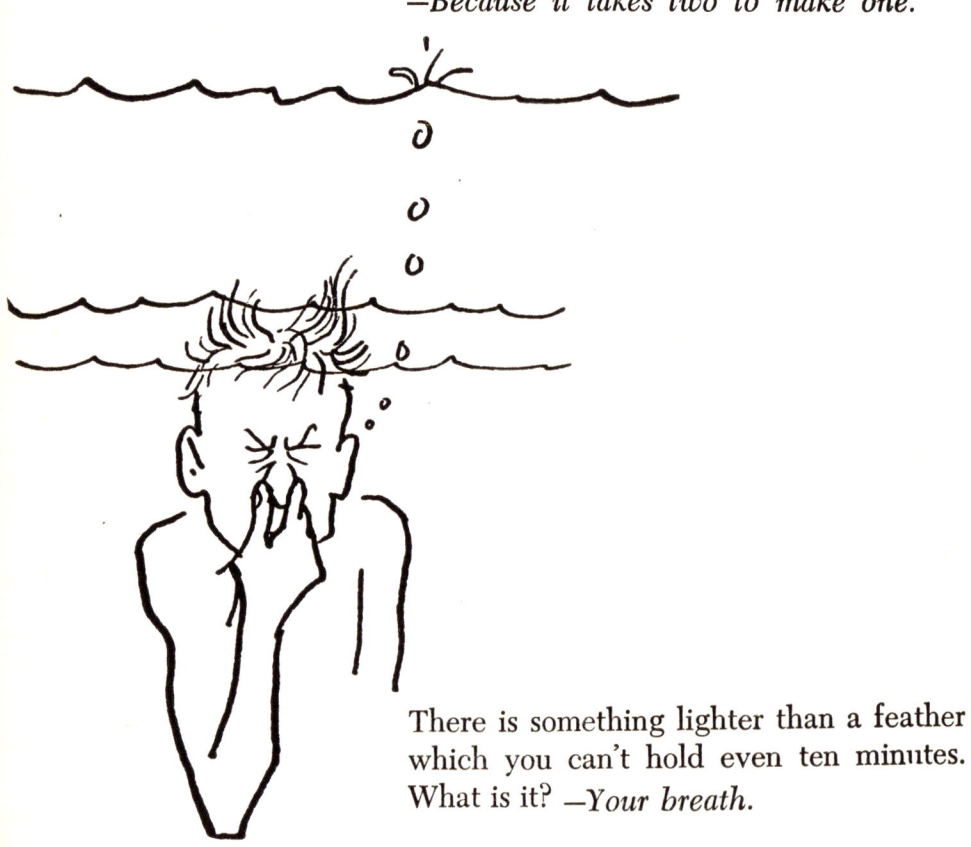

There is something lighter than a feather which you can't hold even ten minutes. What is it? —*Your breath.*

*If a well-known animal you behead,
A larger one you will have instead.*
—F-ox.

What insect do blacksmiths make?
—*They make the fire-fly.*

What are the three swiftest means of communication?
—*Telephone, telegraph and tell a secret.*

Why did the man take a bale of hay to bed?
—*To feed his nightmare.*

When did the fly fly?
—*When the spider spied 'er.*

If you count twenty houses on your right going to school, and twenty on your left coming home, how many houses in all have you counted?
—*Twenty. You counted the same houses going and coming.*

What is neither inside the house nor outside the house, but the house wouldn't be complete without it?
—*Window.*

YOUR BODY

What flowers do you always wear?—*Tulips* (*two lips*).

What do you have that a pin also has?—*A head.*

What part of you is a tropical tree?—*Your palm.*

What do you have that carpenters use?—*Nails.*

What part of you grows on a tree?—*Limbs.*

What animal do you have that dogs like to chase?
—*Hair* (*hare*).

What do you have that every hill has?—*A brow.*

What strongbox do you always carry?—*Your chest.*

What do you have that every soldier carries?—*Arms.*

What do you have that can be found in every yard?
—*A foot.*

What do you have that every river has?—*A mouth.*

What do you have that a bottle has?—*A neck.*

*Look into my face and I'm everybody;
Scratch my back and I'm nobody.
Who am I?*

—A mirror.

What would happen to you if you swallowed your cereal spoon?

—*You wouldn't be able to stir.*

What part of a locomotive is most sensitive?

—*The "tender" part.*

When is a horse like a house?

—*When it has blinds on.*

If a boy broke his knee, where could he get a new one?

—*At the butcher's, when they sell kid knees (kidneys).*

Why should a man's hair turn gray before his moustache?

—*Because it is older.*

What kind of beans won't grow in the garden?

—*Jelly beans.*

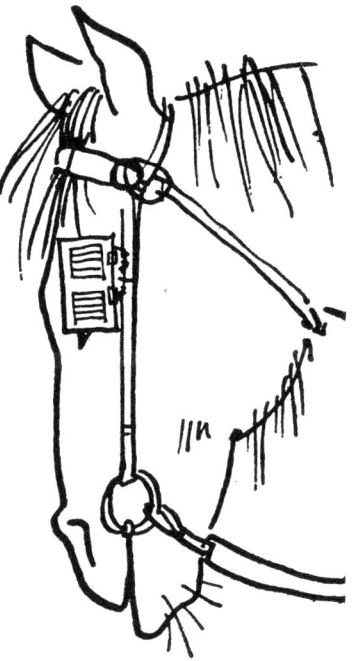

A milk-white bird
Floats down through the air;
And never a tree
But he lights there.
—Snow.

Why are alligators such deceitful creatures?

—*Because they take you in with an open countenance.*

What is the smallest room in the world?

—*A mushroom.*

What is the largest room in the world?

—*The room for improvement.*

Can you turn a melon into a squash?

—*Toss any melon up and it will come down* squash!

Along the Mississippi the mosquitos are so large that a good many of them weigh a pound. They sit on the logs and bark when people go by. Can this be true?

—*Yes, if you caught enough of them they would weigh a pound, and the logs where they sit have bark.*

What word do children always pronounce wrong?

—*Wrong.*

Big at the bottom, little at the top,
A thing in the middle goes flippity-flop.
—A churn.

I fell off a hundred-foot ladder without getting hurt? Why?
—*I fell off the first rung.*

If a man sees eight crows on a limb and shoots three, how many are left?
—*Three. The rest fly away.*

When does a man wear a large watch?
—*When he wants to have a big time.*

Why does an Indian chief wear feathers on his head?
—*To keep his wig warm (wigwam).*

What is the difference between honey and a black eye?
—*One comes from a laboring bee, and the other from a belaboring.*

Those that have eyes have no heads;
Those that have heads have no eyes.
What are they?
—*Needles and pins.*

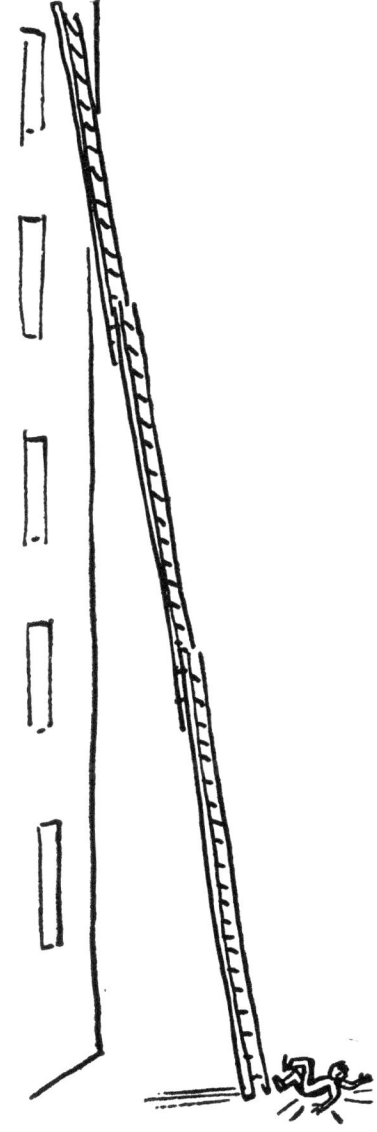

FUNNY LETTERS

Spell mousetrap in three letters.—C, A, T.
Spell dried grass in three letters.—H, A, Y.
Spell hard water in three letters.—I, C, E.
Spell black water in three letters.—I, N, K.
Spell donkey in three letters.—Y, O, U.
What three letters turn children into grownups?—A, G, E.
Spell butter in four letters.—G, O, A, T.
If the whole alphabet were invited to a party, when would the last six letters start?—*After T (tea)*.
Why is A like a honeysuckle?
   —*It always has a B (bee) following it.*
When did Chicago begin with a C and end with an E?
   —*Always.*
What always ends everything?—*The letter G.*
What seven letters did the little girl say when she found the icebox empty?—O, I, C, U, R, M, T.
How do you spell blind pig?
   —B, L, N, D, P, G. You have to spell it that way because a blind pig has no eyes.

Read the following:

      Y Y U R
      Y Y U B
      I C U R
      Y Y 4 me

Too wise you are
Too wise you be
I see you are
Too wise for me.

Has legs like a jumping jack
And ears like a mule,
A tail like a cotton boll,
And runs like a fool.
—A rabbit.

When did the ocean roar the loudest?
—*When it found crabs in its bed.*

When are potatoes like cowboys?
—*When they are shooting from the eyes.*

Why don't doctors become seasick?
—*They are all used to see sickness.*

If you pull it it's a cane, but if you push it it's a tent—what is it?
—*An umbrella.*

Why can't you whisper in school?
—*It's not aloud.*

What goes down to the cellar with four legs and comes back with eight?
—*A cat when she catches a mouse down there.*

A SONG RIDDLE

I had four brothers over the sea.
    Perrie, Merrie, Dixie, Dominie.
And they each sent a present unto me.
    Petrum, Partrum, Paradise, Temporie,
    Perrie, Merrie, Dixie, Dominie.

The first sent a chicken without any bones;
The second sent a cherry without any stones.

The third sent a book which no man could read;
The fourth sent a blanket without any thread.

How could there be a chicken without any bones?
How could there be a cherry without any stones?

How could there be a book which no man could read?
How could there be a blanket without any thread?

Answer:
When the chicken's in the eggshell, there are no bones;
When the cherry's in the blossom, there are no stones;

When the book's in the press no man it can read;
When the wool is on the sheep's back, there is no thread.

    Petrum, Partrum, Paradise, Temporie,
    Perrie, Merrie, Dixie, Dominie.

A man with no arms shot a bird;
A man with no eyes saw it fall;
A man with no legs ran to get it;
A man with no clothes put it in his pocket.
　　　　—That's just a big lie!

How can you make slow horses fast?
—*Tie them up.*

What kind of ears do engines have?
—*They have engineers.*

When do boats become very affectionate?
—*When they hug the shore.*

Why are ships untruthful?
—*Because they lie at every wharf they come to.*

If an egg came floating down the middle of the Hudson River, where would it come from?
—*From a hen.*

What word becomes shorter when you add a syllable to it.
—*Short.*

Humpty Dumpty sat on a wall;
Humpty Dumpty had a great fall.
All the king's horses and all the king's men
Couldn't put Humpty together again.
—An egg.

Are bees good at argument?
—*Yes, a bee always carries its point.*

What kind of umbrella does the President's wife carry on a rainy day?
—*A wet one.*

What makes the best eavesdropper?
—*An icicle.*

What is it that everything in the world has?
—*A name.*

IN THE MIDDLE

What is the happiest vowel?
—*I, because it's in the middle of bliss.*

Why is an island like the letter T?
—*Because it's in the middle of water.*

Why is the letter A like noon?
—*Because it's in the middle of day.*

Why is the letter U never serious?
—*Because it's in the midst of fun.*

What is the center of gravity?—*V.*

*Upon a bridge I saw Uncle Jack,
Walking along with the world on his back.*
—A terrapin.

Why should we never gossip in the stable?

—*Because all horses carry tails (tales).*

What is it that somebody else has to take before you can get it?

—*Your picture.*

If you crawled into a hole bored clear through the earth, where would you finally come out?

—*Out of the hole.*

When should a baker stop baking doughnuts?

—*When he gets tired of the hole business.*

What runs all around the cow pasture, yet never moves?

—*The fence.*

*A little white fence that's always wet,
But never has been rained on yet.*
—The teeth.

What cat do you always find in a library?
—*A cat-a-logue.*

Why does the engine obey the engineer?
—*Because it's afraid of the switches.*

Why are clocks so shy?
—*Because they always hold their hands before their faces.*

Why do you never see a single whole day?
—*Because each day begins by breaking.*

If you fell downstairs, what would you fall against?
—*Against your wishes.*

Where does Friday come before Thursday?
—*In the dictionary.*

Without a bridle or a saddle,
Across a thing I ride astraddle.
And those I ride, by help of me,
Though almost blind, are made to see.
—Spectacles.

Why is a horse like a bird?
—*Didn't you ever see a horse-fly?*

What is the difference between an umbrella and a talkative friend?
—*You can shut the umbrella up.*

What is the easiest way to swallow a door?
—*Bolt it.*

When is a pig like a tree?
—*When it roots.*

Why are crows never cowardly?
—*Because they never show a white feather.*

What has four legs and feathers, and is neither animal nor bird?
—*A featherbed.*

Adam and Eve and Pinch-me
Went down to the river to bathe;
Adam and Eve got drownd-ed.
Which one of the three was saved?
—*The one who answers gets pinched.*

Why is it so profitable to keep hens?
—*Because they give a peck for every grain they eat.*

Are all fishermen stingy?
—*Yes, their business makes them selfish (sell fish).*

Why does a rooster cross the road?
—*To get to the other side.*

What trees are most useful at night?—*Shoe trees.*

TRANSFORMATIONS

When is a sailor not a sailor?
—*When he's a-board.*

When is a door not a door?
—*When it is a-jar.*

When is a baby not a baby?
—*When it's a little cross.*

When is a hat not a hat?
—*When it becomes a woman.*

When is a cat not a cat?
—*When it's a kitten.*

When is a cow not a cow?
—*When it turns into a pasture.*

When is a boy not a boy?
—*When he's a little horse (hoarse).*

*A five-letter word as hard as bone;
Take two away and leave only one.*
                    —St-one.

Would you rather have an elephant chase you or a gorilla?
—*I'd rather have him chase the gorilla.*

What insect is as intelligent as a talking horse?
—*A spelling bee.*

What should a man know before trying to teach tricks to a dog?
—*More than the dog.*

Who always goes to bed with his shoes on?
—*A horse.*

What's the difference between a tunnel and an ear trumpet?
—*A tunnel gets "hollered" out, while an ear trumpet gets "hollered" in.*

What goes round and round the house
And leaves a black glove in the window?
—*Rain.*

NUMBERS

There are three of us in two,
Five of us in seven,
Four of us in nine
And seven in eleven.
—*Letters.*

When do two and two make more than four?
—*When they make 22.*

What number is larger when you turn it upside down?
—*6 becomes 9.*

If a lollipop and a half costs a cent and a half, what will five lollipops cost?
—*Five cents.*

How many nines between 1 and 100?—*Twenty.*

How can four nines equal 100?
—*When written* 99 9/9.

Add two figures to nine and still have less than ten.
—*9 1/2.*

ROMAN NUMERALS

Add ten to nothing and get a large animal.
—*OX.*

Take ten from nine and leave only yourself.
I (X).

Take two letters away from a four-letter word and have four left. Take away another letter and have five left.
—*(F) IV (E); (I) V.*

*I washed my hands in water
That never rained nor run;
I dried them on a towel
That was never wove nor spun.*

—Dew and sun.

Why does a cat rest best in summer?
—*Because summer brings the cat-er-pil-lar.*

When is it correct to serve milk in a saucer?
—*When you feed the cat.*

What always comes into the house through the keyhole?
—*The key.*

When is an owl like a President?
—*When he's a-blinkin' (Abe Lincoln).*

If I were in the sun and U were out of the sun, what bad thing would the sun be?
—*Sin.*

What flies high and low—it has no feet yet it wears shoes?
—*Dust.*

> *What has*
> *Two lookers,*
> *Two hookers,*
> *Four down-hangers,*
> *Four up-standers,*
> *And a fly-swatter?*
>
> —A cow.

What most resembles a hen stealin'?
—A cock robin.

> Why is a half-moon heavier than a full moon?
> —Because the full moon is lighter.

What are stage buildings made of?
—Sham-rocks.

> What burns longer, a red candle or a white one?
> —Both burn shorter.

Why should you always remain calm when you encounter cannibals?
—It's better not to get into a stew.

> To what question must you always answer yes?
> —What does Y, E, S, spell?

> *Round as a doughnut,*
> *Busy as a bee,*
> *Prettiest little thing*
> *You ever did see.*
>
>   —A watch.

What is the best way to hide a bear?
—*Skin him.*

> When are boys most like bears?
> —*When they are "bear"-footed.*

What is the best way to make pants last?
—*Make the coat and vest first.*

> What is the difference between a **hungry** man and a greedy man?
> —*One longs to eat and other eats too long.*

To what question may you never answer yes?
—*Are you asleep?*

FOOLISH ARITHMETIC

What coin doubles in value when you take away half?
 —*A half dollar.*

If you add a father, a mother and a baby, what do you get?
 —*Two and one to carry.*

When is a boy adding numbers like a lame dog?
 —*When he puts down three and carries one.*

How can you prove that a horse has six legs?
 —*Every horse has four legs (forelegs) in front and two behind.*

Do you say, "Nine and five *is* thirteen," or "Nine and five *are* thirteen"?
 —*Nine and five are fourteen.*

How can you show that two times ten equals two times eleven?
 —*Two times ten is twenty and two times eleven is twenty-two (twenty, too).*

If you can buy six eggs for twenty-six cents, how many can you buy for a cent and a quarter?
 —*Six. (A cent and a quarter make twenty-six cents.)*

If two's company and three's a crowd, what are four and five?—*Nine.*

If you had twenty sick chickens and one died, how many would you have left?
 —*Nineteen. (Your hearer probably thought you said twenty-six.)*

How can you divide six apples evenly among four large boys and one small one?
 —*Make apple sauce.*

*Goes North, West, East, and South,
Has a hundred teeth but no mouth.*
—A saw.

Why are horses such pessimistic animals?
—*Because they only know how to say nay (neigh).*

When does a man become two men?
—*When he is beside himself.*

Why are winter trees like boring visitors?
—*It seems so long before they will leave.*

Why don't women grow bald as men do?
—*Because they wear their hair longer.*

What is the least dangerous kind of robbery?
—*Safe robbery.*

If a room with four corners has a cat in each corner, three cats before each cat, and a cat sitting on each cat's tail, how many cats are there in all?
—*Four.*

*From house to house he goes,
A messenger small and slight;
And whether it rains or snows,
He sleeps out all the night.*

      —A path.

Three copycats were sitting on a cliff and one jumped off. How many were left?
—*None, because they were all copycats.*

When is a blackberry not a black berry?
—*When it is green.*

What would a goat do in an old lady's china shop?
—*Butter-cups.*

What can you break with a whisper more easily than with a hammer?
—*A secret.*

What is the difference between candle-light in a cave and a dance at an inn?
—*One is a taper in a cavern and the other is a caper in a tavern.*

What is the most troublesome table in the world?
—*The multiplication table.*

Big at both ends
Small in the middle
Digs up the dirt
And sings like a fiddle.
—Dirt dauber.

Why did the lobster blush?
—*Because it saw the salad dressing.*

What part of New York is in Chicago?
—*The letter O.*

Why is a baseball team like a cake?
—*Both need a good batter.*

When does the rain become too friendly with a girl?
—*When it begins to patter (pat 'er) on the back.*

What is black and white and read all over?
—*A newspaper.*

TEASING QUESTIONS

Did you ever hear the story about two holes in the ground?
—*Well, well.*

Did you ever hear the story of the red hot poker?
—*You couldn't grasp it.*

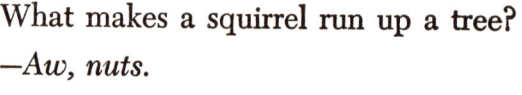

What makes a squirrel run up a tree?
—*Aw, nuts.*

Did you ever hear the story of the new roof?
—*It's over your head.*

What makes a cat walk softly?
—*Oh, rats!*

Did you ever hear the story of the dirty window?
—*You couldn't see through it.*

QUESTIONS WITHOUT ANSWERS

Which comes first, the chicken or the egg?
Which goes through a plank first, the bullet or the hole?
Where does a pig's squeal go when he dies?
Where does your lap go when you stand up?

*I can throw an egg against a wall,
And it will neither break nor fall.
Explain that!*
—The wall won't break nor fall!

What is the very worst weather for rats and mice?
—When it rains cats and dogs.

Why do potatoes grow so fast?
—Because they have eyes and can see where they are going.

Why is coffee like a farmer's best field?
—Because it is good ground.

Where can you lie without being scolded?
—In bed.

What is the difference between a crown prince and the water in a fountain?
—One is heir to the throne and the other is thrown to the air.

How much dirt is there in a hole exactly one foot deep and one foot across?
—None.

*What is higher than a house,
Yet smaller than a mouse?*
—A star.

Why is a snoring boy like a horse jumping a fence?

—Because he does it in his sleep (*in his leap*).

If you threw a gray rock into the sea, what would it become?

—*Wet.*

Why is a nail in a board like a sick person?

—*Both are in-firm.*

Why are potatoes like mended trousers?

—*Because you see them in patches.*

What is the difference between the sun and a loaf of bread?

—*The sun rises from the East and the bread rises from the yeast.*

When is it easiest to read in the woods?

—*When autumn turns the leaves.*

*A riddle, a riddle, as I suppose,
A thousand eyes and never a nose.*
—Flour sifter.

Why does a dog turn round three times before lying down?
—Because one good turn deserves another.

Why does the ocean get angry?
—Because so many people cross it.

Do you know something that would tickle everybody?
—Yes, a feather.

Why is an oyster unlike a small child?
—You have to take the oyster out of its bed to tuck it in.

How did the woodchopper request his tree to fall?
—He just "axed" it.

What has a neck but no head?
—A bottle.

RIDDLES OF LONG AGO

In open field I cannot lie,
And yet I may rest quietly
Within a box of ivory.
　　　　—*A feather on a windy day.*

How far is it round the world?
—*A day's journey for the sun.*

How deep is the sea?
—*Only a stone's throw.*

How far is it from earth to heaven?
—*Only as far as you can see.*

What do crows do when they are three years old?
—*Start their fourth year.*

How many leaves are there on a tree?
—*As many as there are stems for.*

How heavy is the earth?
—*Carry away all the stones and I will weigh it.*

How long should a man's legs be?
—*Long enough to reach the ground.*

How many hairs are there in your head?
—*As many as there are in a donkey's tail. If you do not believe it, we will pluck them one by one from each until we know.*

What is mind?
—*No matter.*

What is matter?
—*Never mind.*

· 82 ·

Red and blue and delicate green;
The king can't catch it and neither can the queen.
Pull it in the room and you can catch it soon.
Answer this riddle by tomorrow at noon.
—Rainbow.

If a dog lost his tail, where should he go to get another one?
—*To a big store where they retail everything.*

Why do milkmen have white horses?
—*To pull their wagons.*

When does a boxer's eye look like a barrel?
—*When it gets bunged up.*

When are waves like balloons?
—*When the wind blows them up.*

Why is the Fourth of July like cheese?
—*We enjoy it better with crackers.*

What has no body, but if it loses an eye has nothing left but a nose?
—*The word noise.*

NUTS

What nut do you eat with bread and jam?—BUTTER*nut*

What nut is like a sneeze?—CASHEW *nut*

What nut do you hang a picture on?—WAL*nut*

What nut makes a good trunk?—CHEST*nut*

What nut do you find at the seashore?—BEECH*nut*

What nut is a green vegetable?—PEA*nut*

What nut is a large nation?—BRAZIL *nut*.

What nut can light a room?—CANDLE*nut*.

What nut is a girl's name?—HAZEL*nut*.

What nut is a pleasant beverage?—COCOA*nut*.

What nut has a hole in the middle?—DOUGH*nut*.

Long legs and short thighs
A bald head and bullet eyes.
—A frog.

When is a yellow dog most likely to enter a house?
—*When the door is open.*

What bad thing does a good tailor do to all his customers?
—*He gives them all fits.*

What is it whose work is only to play?
—*A fountain in a park.*

Is it ever pleasant to receive a blow?
—*Yes, if someone strikes you agreeably.*

How can you push an egg through a finger ring without breaking it?
—*Stick your finger through the ring and push carefully.*

You haven't got it, and you don't want it—but if you had it you wouldn't take the world for it. What is it?
—*A bald head.*

I have a blanket I can't fold,
An apple I can't cut,
And so much money I can't count it.
　　　　　　　—Sky, moon and stars.

What kind of a doctor would a duck become?
—*A quack doctor.*

Why does a freight car need no locomotive?
—*Because the freight makes the car-go.*

What can neither think nor speak, yet tells everybody the truth?
—*A good pair of scales.*

What goes round every tree in the wood and yet never goes into the wood?
—*Bark.*

Why is a pig in the house like a house afire?
—*Because the sooner it is put out the better.*

> *Green skin, red meat,*
> *Full of sugar, hard to beat.*
> —Watermelon.

Why are frogs such delicate animals?
—*Because they croak so easily.*

> When is a bump on your head like a hat on your head?
> —*When it is felt.*

Why is a straw hat like a kiss over the telephone?
—*Because neither is felt.*

> What has a foot on each end and one in the middle?
> —*A yardstick.*

How can you tell a thief from a church bell?
—*One steals from the people and the other peals from the steeple.*

> What runs round and round the house and sneaks in through the keyhole?
> —*The wind.*

Around the corner there is a tree:
Under the tree there is a schoolhouse;
In the schoolhouse there is a desk,
And on the desk there is a bell.
What is the teacher's name?

—Isabel.

Why is a theater such a sad place?
 —*Because all the seats are in tears (tiers).*

What are the coldest seats in a theater?
 —*Those in Z-row.*

Why are clouds like people riding horseback?
 —*Because they hold the rains (reins).*

What's the difference between an empty tube and a foolish Dutchman?
 —*One is a hollow cylinder and the other is a silly Hollander.*

CHAIN ANSWERS

Why is a blotter like a lazy dog?
 —*A blotter is an ink-lined plane; an inclined plane is a slope up; and a slow pup is a lazy dog.*

Why is the wind blind?
 —*The wind is a breeze; a breeze is a zephyr; a zephyr is a yarn; a yarn is a tale; a tail is an appendage; an appendage is an attachment; an attachment is love; and love is blind.*

*Goes over all the hills and hollows,
Bites hard, but never swallows.*
—Frost.

Why can't you trust a bee?
—*Because it's a humbug.*

What is the longest word in the dictionary?
—*Smiles. There's a mile between the first and last letters.*

What should you always keep because nobody else wants it?
—*Your temper.*

Why are trees so polite?
—*Because they always bow (bough) before leaving.*

What is the difference between a barber and the mother of several children?
—*A barber has razors to shave; a mother has shavers to raise.*

What gallops down the road on its head?
—*A horseshoe nail.*

What happened when a lady met a goat in her pantry?
—*The goat turned to butter (butt 'er).*

Has a head but can't think;
Goes to the creek but can't drink.
—A horseshoe nail.

What is the hardest key to turn?
—*A don-key.*

Why do carpenters disbelieve in stone?
—*Because they never saw it.*

When did George Washington first ride in a taxicab?
—*When he took a hack at the cherry tree.*

What happened to the lady who sat on a flagpole to reduce?
—*She fell off.*

It has a head like a cat, feet like a cat and a tail like a cat, but it isn't a cat. What is it?
—*A kitten.*

What stands on one leg with its heart in its head?
—*A cabbage.*

*England, Ireland, Scotland, Wales,
Monkeys, rats, and wiggle-tails.
Spell that in four letters.*
　　　　—T, H, A, T.

When do cows have eight feet?
—*When two cows are together.*

Why are the prairies so flat?
—*Because the sun sets on them every night.*

Why is K like a pig's tail?
—*Because you find it at the end of pork.*

Why is the highest apple on a tree the best one?
—*Because it's the tip-top apple.*

What happens to a man who starts home to dinner and misses his train?
—*He catches it after he gets home.*

What can you hold in your left hand that you can't hold in your right hand?
—*Your right elbow.*

ADAM AND EVE

Who was the fastest runner in history?
—*Adam. He was first in the human race.*

When was Adam created?—*Just a little before Eve.*
What was the longest day that Adam passed?
—*The day that had no Eve in it.*

Did Adam and Eve ever have a date?
—*No, they had an apple.*

What did Adam and Eve lack that everybody else in the world has had?
—*Parents.*

When did Adam and Eve have their biggest quarrel?
—*When they raised Cain.*

Why did Adam bite the apple?
—*Because he had no knife.*

Why did Adam and Eve have no molasses for their biscuits?
—*They tried to raise Cain before they got Abel.*

How long did Cain dislike his brother?
—*As long as he was Abel.*

What three words did Adam use when he introduced himself to Eve, which read the same backwards and forwards?
—*Madam, I'm Adam.*

*What goes into the water, clink clink!
Bends down, but does not drink?*
—A cowbell.

What has eighty-eight keys but can't unlock a single door?
—*A piano.*

Why isn't your nose twelve inches long?
—*If it were, it would be a foot.*

Where do little ears of corn come from?
—*The stalk brings them.*

When does a timid boy turn to stone?
—*When he becomes a little bolder (boulder).*

How do we know that phonographs have been to jail?
—*Because they all have records.*

What comes with a car, goes with a car, is of no use to a car, yet a car can't run without it?
—*Noise.*

White as snow, it's not snow;
Green as grass, it's not grass;
Red as fire, it's not fire;
Black as ink, it's not ink.
What is it?
—A blackberry.

Why is a dog biting his tail a very good manager?

—Because he shows he is able to make both ends meet.

When are electricians most successful?

—When they make good connections.

What would be the worst vegetable to take aboard ship?

—A leek (leak).

Why did the woodchopper's daughter never marry?

—Nobody ever "axed" her.

There were 710 men on a boat that turned over. What was left?

—OIL.

What can turn without moving?

—Milk—it can turn sour.

Whitey saw Whitey in Whitey.
Whitey sent Whitey to drive
Whitey out of Whitey.

—Mr. White sent a white dog to drive a white cow out of his cotton field.

What tie should a fashionable pig wear to a dance?

—*He should wear his "pig's tie" (pigsty).*

When is a pianist like a jailor?
—*When he fingers his keys.*

What does everybody do when it rains?
—*Let it rain.*

Why did the fat man praise everybody after a car ran over him?
—*Because the accident made him flatter.*

What's the difference between a cat and a match?

—*A match lights on its head, but a cat lights on its feet.*

Which weighs more, a pound of feathers or a pound of lead?
—*They weigh the same.*

SPELLING RIDDLES

Spell Mississippi:
M, I, double letter,
I, double letter,
I, humpback, humpback, I.

Spell Cincinnati:
A needle and a pin,
Spell Cin, cin, cin;
A gnat and a fly
Spell CINCINNATI.

Spell Bullfrog:

B, U, hippety,
L, L, croak and crunk;
F, R, splash,
And O, G, sunk!

Spell Pumpkin:

P, U, umpkin, umpkin I;
P, U, umpkin, umpkin, PUMPKIN PIE.

Spell Bumblebee:

B, U, umble, umble E;
B, U, bumble, BUMBLE BEE.

Spell Woodpecker:

W, double O, D, wood;
Sockety peck.
Run round the limb
And stick your bill in
WOODPECKER!

Spell Constantinople:

Can you count?
Can you stand?
Can you Constant-I?
Can you nople?
Can you pople?
Can you CONSTANTINOPLE!

As soft as silk, as white as milk,
As bitter as gall, a thick wall,
And a green coat covers me all.
                —A walnut.

Why are fish so well educated?
—*Because they are always found in schools.*

What is the chief difference between land and sea?
—*The land is dirty and the sea is "tidy."*

How could a good fireman lose his job?
—*He might go to blazes too fast.*

When is a man sure to hear knocks in his car?
—*When he has a backseat driver.*

What binds two people together yet touches only one?
—*A wedding ring.*

What is it that more eyes doth wear
Than forty men within the land,
Which glisten as the crystal clear
Against the sun, when they do stand?
——*A peacock's tail.*

Why do little pigs eat so much?
—*To make hogs of themselves.*

Why do people laugh up their sleeves?
—*Because that's where their funnybones are.*

Why is a coward like a leaky barrel?
—*Both run.*

What is big enough to hold a pig and small enough to hold in your hand?
—*A pen.*

How would a crazy teacher resemble an old car without a self-starter?
—*She'd be just a crank surrounded by a lot of little nuts.*

What has four legs and a back but no body?
—*A chair.*

*I walked and walked and at last I got it;
I didn't want it, so I stopped and looked for it;
When I found it I threw it away.
What was it?*

—A thorn in the foot.

Why were the elephants the last animals to leave the Ark?

—*They had to pack their trunks.*

Why is a nobleman like a book?
—*Because he has a title.*

What has four eyes and can't see?
—*The Mississippi River.*

Why is a watch like a vine running round a stump?
—*Because it's a stemwinder.*

Which travels faster, heat or cold?
—*Heat travels faster because you can catch cold.*

My riddle's a bug that has bitten me;
Backwards it's fresh air from the sea.
—*Gnat (tang).*

ADD A LETTER

Why is the letter D so dangerous?
—*Because it makes ma mad.*

What letter would be most helpful to a deaf woman?
—*An H because it would make her ear hear.*

What is the difference between here and there?
—*The letter T.*

Why should boys avoid the letter A after they are grown?
—*Because it makes men mean.*

Why is summer like the letter N?
—*It makes ice nice.*

Why is a teacher of girls like the letter C?
—*She turns lasses into classes.*

Why is the letter B like a hot fire?
—*It makes oil boil.*

What will the letter B do to a narrow road?
—*It will make it broad.*

Why is W the most unfriendly letter?
—*It always makes ill will.*

How can you make a pearl out of a pear?
—*Add L to it.*

Why should a lad avoid the letter Y?
—*It can turn a lad into a lady.*

Why is T the most powerful letter?
—*It can make a star start.*

> *It's true I have both hands and face,*
> *And move before your eyes;*
> *Yet when I go my body stands,*
> *And when I stand I lie.*
>
> *—A clock.*

What is the best way to get a duck for dinner?
—Go jump in the lake.

> Why do girls like to wear ribbons in their hair?
> *—Because they like bows (beaux).*

Which is better to say: "The house burned down" or "The house burned up"?
—Either is bad.

> What can you change oftener than you change your clothes?
> *—Your mind.*

What kind of hen lays the longest?
—A dead hen.

> If you saw a bird sitting in an apple tree, how could you shake an apple down without disturbing the bird?
> *—Wait till he flies away.*

*A hill full, a hole full,
You can't catch a bowl full.*

—Smoke.

When is a turkey like a ghost?
—*When he's a goblin (a-gobblin').*

What does an envelope say when you lick it?
—*It just shuts up and says nothing.*

Why is the sun like good bread?
—*It isn't light until after it rises.*

What coat has no buttons and must be put on wet?
—*A coat of paint.*

What's the difference between an auction and seasickness?
—*One is a sale of effects and the other is effects of a sail.*

What is the most useful and least thought-of thing in the kitchen?
—*Dishrag.*

Long man legless
Came to the door staffless;
More afraid of a rooster and a hen
Than of a dog and forty men.

—A worm.

Why would it be insulting if a rooster paid you a compliment?
—*Because he could only say it in fowl language.*

Why is a sculptor an unhappy man?
—*Because he makes faces and busts.*

If a boy wears his pants out before noon, what should he do?
—*Wear them back in.*

What is the difference between a gardener and a billiard player?
—*One minds his peas and the other minds his cues.*

What do bees do with all their honey?
—*They cell it.*

What shoemaker makes shoes without using any leather?
—*A horseshoer makes horseshoes.*

MUSICAL NONSENSE

Name an organ without a stop. —*Your tongue!*

What is the best way for children to act?
—*They should B-natural.*

What musical key makes a good officer?
—*A-Major.*

What musical key can't vote?—*A-Minor.*

Why are ghosts like songs?
—*They usually appear in sheets.*

What is musical about an icy sidewalk?
—*You must C-sharp or you'll B-flat.*

What musical instrument is your nose?
—*It's an organ on your face.*

What large instruments do you carry in your ears?
—*Drums.*

What instrument should we never believe?
—*A lyre (liar).*

When do people eat a large musical instrument?
—*When they have a piano for tea (pianoforte).*

If a church catches fire, why does the organ always burn up?
—*Because the firehose can't play on it.*

What is the most musical grandfather a child could have?
—*One who fiddles with his beard.*

In marble walls as white as milk,
Lined with a skin as soft as silk;
Within a fountain crystal clear
A golden apple doth appear.
There are no gates to this stronghold,
Yet thieves break in and steal the gold.

—An egg.

What is the difference between a sigh and a monkey?

—*A sigh means Oh, dear—and a monkey means you, dear!*

Why is a window in the roof like the sun?

—*Because it's a skylight.*

Which is the reddest side of an apple?
—*The outside.*

When is a rower like an Indian chief?
—*When he feathers his scull.*

Why are pianos so noble?

—*Because they are upright, square and grand.*

What has two tongues and no mouth?
—*A pair of shoes.*

Hoddy Toddy
Has a round body
Three feet and an iron hat.
Now what do you make of that?

—An iron pot.

What kind of a dog has no tail?

—*A hot dog.*

Why are grown people lazier than children?

—*Because they lie longer in bed.*

Why is a paper dollar more valuable than a silver dollar?

—*Because you double it every time you put it into your pocket.*

What is the difference between a milkmaid and a seagull?

—*One skims the milk and the other skims the water.*

What is higher without a head than with a head?

—*A pillow.*

Goes up and down the street, can't walk;
Goes to the river, can't drink;
Goes to the barn, can't sleep.
—A wagon.

If five cats catch five mice in five minutes, how long will it take one cat to catch a mouse?
—*Five minutes.*

Why is snow like an apple tree?
—*Because it leaves in the spring.*

When a carpenter starts a new house, where does he strike the first nail?
—*On the head.*

What is the difference between a boy and a postage stamp?
—*A stamp can be licked only once.*

What becomes less and less tired the more it works?
—*A car wheel.*

What is neither inside the house nor outside the house and the house can't do without it?
—*Window.*

NECK RIDDLES

A *neck riddle* is one in which a condemned person saves his neck by asking a riddle nobody can answer.

UNDER GRAVEL*

A man was condemned to be hanged and was riding horseback to the gallows with his hangmen. They offered to spare his life if he could think up a riddle none of them could answer. At the gallows he asked, without dismounting:

> *Under gravel I do travel,*
> *On oak leaves I do stand;*
> *I ride my pony and never fear;*
> *I hold my bridle in my hand.*

After everybody had tried to guess, he showed them that he had put gravel in his hat and oak leaves in his boots. With this riddle he won his life.

LOVE

> On Love I sit, on Love I stand;
> Love I hold within my hand.
> I love Love and Love loved me;
> Love is dead in Tennessee.

—A girl had a dog named Love. When it died, she worked bits of its hair into her cushion, her shoe and her glove.

---

* Grateful acknowledgment is made to Vance Randolph and Columbia University Press for "Under Gravel," which is summarized from the story "Under Gravel I Do Travel" in Vance Randolph: *Who Blowed up the Church House?* Columbia University Press, N. Y., 1952.

Brownie, Brownie upstairs,
Brownie, Brownie downstairs;
If you don't watch out,
Brownie, Brownie'll bite you.
—A wasp.

Why is your heart like a policeman?
—*Because it follows a regular beat.*

What should you do if you found a horse in the bathtub?
—*Pull the plug out.*

When is an apple like a comic book?
—*When it is red (read).*

When does a dog look like a boy?
—*Whenever he takes after one.*

What two animals do you always take to bed with you?
—*Your calves.*

Is there much difference between the North Pole and the South Pole?
—*Yes, all the difference in the world.*

*Runs and runs, but never walks;
Has a long tongue, but never talks.*

—A wagon.

Why is a lazy young dog like a hill?
—*Because he's a slow pup (slope up).*

When do your nose and chin quarrel?
—*Whenever words pass between them.*

What makes more noise than a pig caught in a fence?
—*Two pigs.*

What has panes and doesn't ache?
—*A window.*

Why is it dangerous to walk about in the spring?
—*Because then the grass is full of blades, every flower has its pistil, and all the trees are shooting.*

What food is made from flowers?
—*Honey.*

Opens like a barn door,
Shuts up like a trap;
Guess all your life,
You'll never guess that.
—Scissors.

How should a parrot always speak?

—*He should always speak in polysyllables (Polly Syllables).*

What did most American men and women used to be?

—*American boys and girls.*

What will always bear looking into once more?

—*A mirror.*

What horse can see as well behind as he does in front?

—*A blind horse.*

What is the difference between an apple and a pretty girl?

—*One you squeeze to get cider, and the other you have to get 'side 'er to squeeze.*

BIBLE QUIZ

Who is the first man mentioned in the Bible?
—Chap. I.

What is the first mention of pork in the Bible?
—*When they took Ham into the Ark.*

When was money first mentioned in the Bible?
—*When a dove brought the green-back to Noah.*

When did Moses sleep five in a bed?
—*When he slept with his forefathers (four fathers).*

How do we know that whales can be very deceptive?
—*Because one took Jonah in.*

How do we know that Sampson was a good actor?
—*Because he brought down the house.*

What did Lot's wife turn to before she turned to salt?
—*She turned to rubber.*

Was Goliath surprised when David hit him with the stone?
Yes. Such a thing had never entered his head before.

What animals brought the most and the least luggage into the Ark?—*The elephant brought his trunk and the rooster brought only his comb.*

Brown I am and much admired,
Many horses have I tired;
I tire a horse and weary a man.
Guess this riddle if you can.
—A saddle.

What never asks a question yet often has to be answered?
—*The telephone.*

What is the difference between a sewing machine and a kiss?
—*One sews seams nice, the other seems so nice.*

A man lost his dog in the woods. How did he find him again?
—*By listening to the bark in the trees.*

Why do birds in a nest always agree?
—*To keep from falling out.*

Why are playing cards like wolves?
—*Because they come in a pack.*

Two brothers we are,
Great burdens we bear,
By which we are bitterly pressed.
In truth we may say,
We are full all the day,
But empty when we go to rest.
—A pair of shoes.

What animal comes from the clouds?
—*The reindeer (the rain, dear!)*

Where is the hardest place to pick a lock?
—*On a bald head.*

What always becomes a woman?
—*A girl.*

Why are railroads so patriotic?
—*Because they are bound to the land with strong ties.*

What should you say to a man who told you he has a lilac bush fifty feet tall?
—*I wish I could lie like (lilac) you.*

What has four wings and flies?
—*Two birds.*

Black without and red within;
Pick up your foot and stick it in.
　　—A boot with a red lining.

What did a girl say to her boy friend who threatened to jump off a high cliff?
—*That's a lot of bluff.*

What flower should be kept in a strong cage?
—*The tiger lily.*

Why does the moon go to the bank?
—*To change quarters.*

What kind of bank has no money?
—*A river bank.*

How can you tell a jeweler from a jailor?
—*One sells watches and the other watches cells.*

What's always running but can't get anywhere?
—*A clock.*

NONSENSE GEOGRAPHY

What is the greatest surgical operation on record?
—*Lansing, Mich.*

What is the greatest task on earth?
—*Wheeling, W. Va.*

What country do you become on a cold morning?
—*Chile.*

Why is the Panama Canal like the u in cucumber?
—*It's between two seas (C's).*

What was the largest island before Australia was discovered?
—*Australia.*

What state is round in both ends and high in the middle?
—*O - hi - O.*

What are the most prosperous islands on earth?
—*The Fortunate Islands.*

Why are the people of Ireland so rich?
—*Their capital is always Dublin (Doublin').*

On what islands should you always find bread and meat?
—*The Sandwich Islands.*

If Miss Issippi gives Miss Ouri her New Jersey, what will Dela Ware?
—*I don't know, but Al-ask-a.*

Flower of England, fruit of Spain,
Met together in a shower of rain,
Put in a bag, tied round with a string.
If you tell me this riddle, I'll give you a ring.
—A plum pudding.

What part of a fish weighs the most?
—*The scales.*

What is the correct height for people to stand?
—*Over two feet.*

Why is a crossword puzzle like a quarrel?
—*Because one word leads to another.*

Which is easier to spell: Fiddle-de-dee, or fiddle-de-dum?
—*Fiddle-de-dee is spelled with more E's.*

What goes most against a farmer's grain?
—*His reaper.*

A farmer said, "If it comes it won't come, but if it doesn't come it will come." Explain that.
—*He was planting grain and meant to say: If the crow comes he'll eat the seed, but if the crow doesn't come, the seed will come up.*

*Long, slim, black fellow,
Pull the trigger and hear him bellow.*
                    —A gun.

Why isn't the moon rich?
—*It spends its quarters getting full.*

How can you make a Maltese cross?
—*Pull its tail.*

How can you buy eggs and be sure they have no chickens in them?
—*Buy duck eggs.*

Why are people never hungry when crossing a desert?
—*Because of the sand which is (sandwiches) there.*

What goes round the woods and pasture, and leaves but one track?
—*A snake.*

Whitey went upstairs,
Whitey came downstairs,
Whitey left Whitey upstairs.

—A white hen went upstairs and laid an egg.

When did beef go the highest?
—*When the old cow jumped over the moon.*

If you were locked up in a room with nothing but a baseball bat, how would you get out?

—*Strike one, strike two, strike three, you're out!*

What is the difference between a good boy and a bad boy?
—*One does as his father says; the other does as his father did.*

If you take away all my letters, I remain the same. Who am I?
—*The postman.*

Why is the Mississippi noisier than most rivers?
—*Because it has more mouths than most.*

When will water stop running downhill?
—*When it reaches the bottom.*

FLOWERS

What flower do cooks use a great deal?
—*Buttercup.*

What flower is a friendly remark at parting?
—*Forget-me-not.*

What flowers will you see in a poultry yard?
—*Phlox (flocks).*

What flower do ladies wear on their feet?
—*Lady's-slippers.*

What flower suggests late afternoon?
—*Four-o'clock.*

What flower reminds one of church?
—*Jack-in-the-pulpit.*

What flower would you see on the clotheslines of Holland?
—*Dutchman's breeches.*

What flower may you see in wintry weather?
—*Snowdrop.*

What flower tells how to get rich quick?
—*Marigold (marry gold).*

What flower tells how to start Junior on an errand?
—*Johnny-jump-up.*

*I have a little house,
And a mouse wouldn't fit in it;
Yet all the men in our town
Couldn't count the windows in it.*

—A thimble.

When is a fish like a bird?
—*When it takes a fly.*

What makes the best slippers in the world?
—*Banana peels.*

How can you eat breakfast without getting up?
—*Just take a couple of rolls in bed.*

What is the difference between a mirror and a boy who chatters nonsense?
—*The mirror reflects without talking and the boy talks without reflecting.*

What can a man give to a woman that he can't give to a man?
—*His name.*

What will stay hot longest in the refrigerator?
—*Pepper.*

*Hickamore, Hackamore,
On the king's kitchen door;
All the king's horses,
And all the king's men,
Couldn't drive Hickamore, Hackamore,
Off the king's kitchen door.*
                    —*Sunshine.*

When is a ship like snow?
—*When it's a-drift.*

Why is a goose like a cow's tail?
—*They both grow down.*

When do your teeth sound just like your tongue?
—*When they chatter.*

What is it from which you may take away the whole and still have some left, or take away some and have the whole left?
—*The word wholesome.*

Could you improve a funny story with a hammer?
—*Yes, you could make it more striking.*

What has two heads, one tail, four legs on one side, and two legs on the other?
—*A woman riding horseback on a side-saddle.*

Over on the hill there is a pony,
Too young to bridle,
Too young to saddle,
Too young to ride.
What's his owner's name? I've told you three times.

—Young.

How do we know that a man galloping up a hill is taking a puppy to his girl friend?
—*Because he's taking a gallop up (a gal a pup).*

Why does a frightened man's hair look like a barrel?
—*Because it stands on end.*

What color does a boy turn if you pinch him?
—*It makes him yellow (yell, "Oh").*

Why does a cow go over a hill?
—*Because she can't go under it.*

What is the difference between a teacher and an engineer?
—*One trains the mind and the other minds the train.*

On the road I met three people. They were neither men, women, nor children. Who were they?
—*A man, a woman and a child.*

TIME RIDDLES

What time is it when you see a monkey scratching a flea with its left hand?
 —*Five after one.*

What time is it when the clock strikes thirteen?
 —*Time to have the clock repaired.*

If a man gave ten cents to his son and fifteen cents to his daughter, what time would it be?
 —*A quarter to two.*

What's the hardest train to catch?
 —*The 12:50; it's ten to one if you catch it.*

At what time is a riddle the funniest?
 —*When it strikes one.*

Why is yesterday like a baseball game?
 —*It's past-time.*

What is always behind time?
 —*The back of a clock.*

Why does time always run away?
 —*It's afraid people will kill it.*

What occurs twice in a moment and not once in a thousand years?
 —*The letter M.*

When is a train whistle like a clock?
 —*When it says toototoo (two to two).*

What do you see twice in every day, four times in every week and only once in a year?
 —*The letter E.*

The land was white,
The seed was black;
It'll take a good scholar
To riddle me that.
     —Paper and ink.

Why did the poultry farmer name his rooster Robinson?
—*Because he Crusoe.*

If it takes a thousand nuts to hold a car together, how many would it take to scatter it?
—*Only one.*

What two keys are too big to carry in your pocket?
—*Mon-key and Don-key.*

Why is it a mistake to put on your shoe?
—*Every time you do you put your foot in it.*

When are a poor man and a rich man in the same station?
—*When they are waiting for a train.*

How can you keep a rooster from crowing on Monday morning?
—*Eat him for Sunday dinner.*

What has four fingers and a thumb,
But has neither flesh nor bone?
    —A glove.

Why are frogs such delicate animals?
—*Because they croak every night.*

Why is a tree like a dog?
—*When it dies it loses its bark.*

What American had the largest family?
—*George Washington. He was the father of his country.*

Why is a sweetheart like a doorknob?
—*Because she's something to adore (a door).*

Why are your eyes like good friends who are separated?
—*Because they correspond but don't meet.*

What has a head and four legs **and only** one foot?
—*A bed.*

What lives in winter,
Dies in summer,
And grows with its root upwards?
              —An icicle.

What animal can go around a button?

—*A goat often goes round a-buttin'.*

Why is your handwriting like a dead pig?
—*Because it's done with the pen.*

When is it easiest to see through a man?

—*When he has a pane (pain) in his stomach.*

In what very surprising places can you find fish?

—*You can find a perch in a birdcage, a skate in a toyshop, and a sole on a shoe.*

What should we give people who are too breezy?

—*The air.*

What goes all the way to town, yet makes just two tracks?

—*A wagon.*

OCCUPATIONS

What workers have their products trampled on by everybody?
—*Shoemakers.*

What is the President's trade?
—*He's a cabinet maker.*

What trade does the sun follow all summer?
—*He's a good tanner.*

What trade does the sun follow only one month a year?
—*In May he's a mason (May son).*

What trade do little tin dogs follow?
—*They're tinkers (tin curs).*

What do broken bones work at?
—*They knit.*

What business would you recommend to a small boy who wants to be bigger?
—*Grocer (grow, sir).*

In what occupation do men cut the best figures?
—*Sculptors cut the best figures.*

What occupation of ancient Rome did the cannibal mention after eating the lady missionary?
—*Gladiator (glad I ate 'er).*

> *Round as an apple,*
> *Shaped like a cup,*
> *All the king's horses*
> *Can't pull it up.*
>
> —A well.

If you sold two small pigs for five dollars, what would a grown hog come to?
—*The feed trough.*

> Why is a dirty boy like flannel?
> —*Because he shrinks from washing.*

When does a boy quit growing taller?
—*When he begins to grow down.*

> What is the difference between a car owner and a little dog's tail?
> —*One keeps a car and other keeps a-waggin'.*

What would happen in the army if a train ran over a peanut?
—*A shell would burst and two kernels would be crushed.*

> How can your pocket be empty and still have something in it?
> —*It can have a hole in it.*

*Above the earth,
Not in a tree.
Now I've told you,
So you tell me!*

    —Knot in a tree.

Why should a fat man always wear a plaid suit?

—*To keep a good check on his stomach.*

A man was locked in a room which had nothing in it except a piano. How did he get out?

—*He played the piano until he found the right key.*

When does a man sneeze three times together?

—*When he has to.*

What could you put into a barrel full of water to make it lighter?

—*Holes.*

> *Riddle me, riddle me, what is that:*
> *Over your head and under your hat?*
> —Hair.

Why should a clock never be put upstairs?
—*It might run down and strike one.*

> Are there any men who have to shave twenty times a day?
> —*Yes, barbers.*

Where are two heads better than one?
—*On a barrel.*

> Why is your hand like a hardware store?
> —*Because it carries nails.*

What should you do if you split your sides laughing?
—*Run till you get a stitch in them.*

> Why is a barefoot boy like an Eskimo?
> —*The barefoot boy wears no shoes and the Eskimo wears snowshoes.*

What has ears but can't hear?
—*A cornstalk.*

WHAT DID THEY SAY?

What did the little chicken say when the old hen laid an orange?
—*Oh, see the orange mar-ma-lade!*

What did the big firecracker say to the little firecracker?
—*My pop is bigger than your pop.*

What did one little inkdrop ask another little inkdrop?
—*Are all your relatives in the pen too?*

What did the rug say to the floor?
—*Hands up! I've got you covered.*

What did the floor say to the wall?
—*I'll meet you at the corner.*

What did the mother strawberry say to the baby strawberry?
—*Junior, you're always getting into a jam.*

What did the apple say to the apple pie?
—*You've got a crust!*

What did one peach say to another?
—*How did we ever get out on such a limb?*

What did the candy bar say to the lollipop?
—*Hello, sucker!*

What did the mayonnaise say to the icebox?
—*Please close the door. I'm dressing.*

What did the big toe say to the little toe?
—*There's a heel following us.*

What did the hen say to her grownup daughter?
—*An egg a day will keep the ax away.*

What did the big rose say to the little rose?
—*Hiya, bud.*

What did Jack Frost say to the rose?
—*Wilt thou?* (*and it wilted*).

It can't go up the chimney up,
But goes up the chimney down;
It can't come down the chimney up,
But comes down the chimney down.
— An umbrella.

Why are sheep in their fold like letters written after supper?
—*Because they are all penned at night.*

What happens to a lighted match if you drop it into a river?
—*It goes out.*

Why is a ringing bell like an onion?
—*Because peal (peel) follows peal.*

What's the difference between a cloud and a spanked child?
—*One pours rain and the other roars with pain.*

What is it that a girl often looks for but hopes never to find?
—*A hole in her stocking.*

*As I went through a field of wheat,
I found something to eat.
'Twas neither fish nor flesh nor bone;
I kept it till it ran alone.*
—An egg.

What is the best way to make peas come up early?
—*Turn hens into the garden.*

When is a cigarette like bacon?
—*When it is smoked.*

What is the difference between a blind man and a retired sailor?
—*The blind man cannot see to go and the retired sailor cannot go to sea.*

What do you take off last before getting into bed?
—*Your feet off the floor.*

Why do you always find a lost object in the very last place you look for it?
—*Because when you find it you stop looking for it.*

RIDDLES ABOUT THE UNITED STATES

What state is an exclamation?
—O.

What state is a number?
—Tenn.

What state is a kind parent?
—Pa.

What state should be the cleanest?
—Wash.

What state saved Noah and his family?
—Ark.

What state suggests poor health?
—Ill.

What state is a good doctor?
—Md.

What state contains the most metal?
—Ore.

What state thinks most of itself?
—Me.

What state is the happiest?
—Ga. (gay)

What state is a grain?
—R.I. (rye)

What two states are the two largest ladies on earth?
—Miss Ouri and Miss Issippi.

What is the bow that has no arrow?
What is the singer that has but one song?
—The rainbow, that never killed a sparrow;
—The cuckoo, who singeth it all the day long.

What happened to the cat that started across a desert on Christmas day?
—*He got sandy claws (Santa Claus).*

Why do people admire aviators?
—*Because they rise so rapidly in the world.*

When do clocks talk the most?
—*When they are well wound up.*

If a tree broke a window, what should the windows say?
—*Tree-mend-us.*

What can you eat that nobody on earth ever saw before?
—*You can break a peanut and eat the kernel.*

What is it that every child spends much time making, yet no one can ever see it when made?
—*Noise.*

*Something lives on yonder hill,
It rocks and rocks and never stands still.*
—A tree.

When an apple wanted to fight a banana, why did the banana run away?
—*Because it was yellow.*

How far can a dog go into the woods?
—*To the center. Then he starts out again.*

Why was the little milkdrop crying?
—*Because all his friends were in the jug.*

What is it that God never sees, a king seldom sees, and most people see every day?
—*An equal.*

What kind of jam do grownups often get caught in?
—*A traffic jam.*

What is the difference between a photographer and the measles?
—*One makes facsimiles and the other makes sick families.*

A man rode to town on Friday;
He stayed there all night
And came back on the same Friday.
How could that be?
—He rode a horse named **Friday**.

Why is a colt like an egg?
—*It can't be used until it is broken.*

What paper should make the best kites?
—*Flypaper.*

Why do hens lay eggs?
—*If they didn't they'd drop them.*

Why does everybody else always have more money in their pockets than you have?
—*Because you have no money in their pockets.*

What begins with P and ends with E and has a thousand letters?
—*Postoffice.*

What has fifty heads but can't think?
—*A box of matches.*

ROUND-THE-WORLD NONSENSE

What land do babies like best?
—*Lapland.*

In what country must doughnuts be fried?
—*In Greece.*

From what country do fish come?
—*From Finland.*

What island do you often mention in greeting a friend?
—*Hawaii. (How are you?)*

What did the mother ask her crying child?
—*Are you Hungary?*

What did the child reply?
—*Yes, Siam.*

What did the mother say next?
—*Come along then, and I'll Fiji.*

What did she give him to eat?
—*A slice of Turkey.*

Why did the child start crying again?
—*He wanted Samoa.*

What did the mother say that time?
—*Stop those Wales!*

> *Mouth like a barn door,*
> *Ears like a cat;*
> *Goes all night*
> *And you can't guess that.*
> —An owl.

What is not a bird yet takes a fly oftener than a bird does?
—*A spider.*

> What is the hardest thing about learning to skate?
> —*The ice.*

What will be yesterday and was tomorrow?
—*Today.*

> Why is a crow like a lawyer?
> —*He likes to have his caws (cause) heard.*

What is bought by the yard and is worn by the foot?
—*A carpet.*

> What can go over the water and through the water without getting wet?
> —*Sunlight.*

FOREIGN RIDDLES

What has wood on both sides and flesh in the middle?

—*A cradle with a baby in it.* (ALBANIA.)

> I have white cattle in my kraal, but one is red. What is that?
>
> —*The teeth and the tongue.* (AFRICA: TONGA.)

What is the white horse that goes into the stable and turns brown?

—*Bread put into an oven.* (AFRICA: KXATLA.)

> What is the large black bird that feeds growing children?
>
> —*A cooking pot.* (AFRICA: KAMBA.)

Who sits down in the king's chair before the king does?

—*A fly.* (AFRICA: WANANWEZI.)

> What are the twins that turn round together but never come together?
>
> —*The ears.* (AFRICA: HAUSA.)

What is the country where all the men wear beards?

—*A cornfield.* (AFRICA: MAKUA.)

> What has a skin like a little camel and ears like a donkey?
>
> —*A rabbit.* (ALGERIA.)

What is the disk floating in the middle of a lake, that nobody can reach?

—*The moon in the sky.* (ANNAM.)

> Who is the lady that sits weeping in a window, whose tears will finally destroy her?
>
> —*A candle burning.* (ARABIA.)

What is the animal often seen going along with eight feet, six ears, three mouths and one tail?

—*A horse carrying two riders.* (ARGENTINA.)

> What is the little house that has many stories and fifty thousand tenants?
>
> —*A beehive.* (PARAGUAY.)

What runs round the house dragging a mop behind it?

—*A cat, with its tail.* (BELGIUM.)

> What is the house that has two windows which close without anyone's touching them?
>
> —*They are the eyes.* (BRAZIL.)

I have eyes but cannot see;
I have ears but cannot hear;
I have lips but cannot speak.
What am I?

—*An icon or religious image.* (BULGARIA.)

I have a mule—a fast runner, but unless
I push him at every step he won't go.
What is that?

—*A needle, pushed with a thimble.*
(CAPE VERDE ISLANDS.)

> I walked and walked around a little
> church, but found no door to enter by.
> What is that?
>
> —*An egg.* (PORTUGAL.)

What is long like a creeper, beautiful as
a flower, of royal caste, and with a deadly
bite?

—*A cobra.* (CEYLON.)

Two hairy ones are dragging along a hairless one while a man hangs onto its tail.
What is that?

—*Oxen, a plow and a plowman.* (CHILE.)

> Two bamboo sticks drive white ducks
> through a narrow door. What is that?
>
> —*Eating rice with chopsticks.* (CHINA.)

In a great plaza filled with people I saw
a violent scene, and the more dangerous
it became, the more the crowd liked it.
What was it?

—*A bullfight.* (CUBA.)

> A little barrel fell off the roof, and no
> cooper can repair it.
>
> —*An egg.* (CZECHOSLOVAKIA.)

People don't cook it or chew it or swallow it, but many people say it tastes good. What is it?
—*Tobacco smoke.* (DENMARK.)

What is the cloth woven without thread that conquers both Turks and Sultans?
—*Sleep.* (EGYPT.)

What is the black mother that wears a white gown?
—*The earth mantled in snow.* (ESTONIA.)

What is dressed up in the daytime, but at night all its finery is put away?
—*The market place.* (ETHIOPIA.)

Who are the two from whom we are always begging and who always give generously?
—*The earth and the sea. The earth gives crops and fruits and the sea gives fish.* (FIJI ISLANDS.)

What dances and plays the whole summer long, but hides its face when winter comes?
—*Water (ice covers it in winter).* (FINLAND.)

Who wears thirty-six petticoats and never had a dressmaker?
—*An onion.* (FRANCE.)

There is a great house that the wind blows over, and those who live inside it cannot speak. What is it?
—*The sea and fish.* (GERMANY.)

What is it that walks if I tie it up and
stops if I untie it?
—*A sandal.* (GREECE.)

> The Riddle of the Sphinx:
> What is it that goes first on four feet,
> then on two feet, and at last on three
> feet?
> —*Man (who crawls as an infant, walks
> upright when grown, and uses a cane when
> old).* (ANCIENT GREECE.)

What is my garden of potatoes that bloom
only at night?
—*The sky and stars.* (HAITI.)

> What is the red cave where soldiers
> stand dressed in white?
> —*The mouth and teeth.* (HAWAII.)

Four sisters chase each other through
the air, but none ever catches up with
another. What is that?
—*The four wings of a windmill.* (HOLLAND.)

> What is both inside and outside the house,
> and is just where it belongs?
> —*The door.* (HUNGARY.)

I'm so unlucky that I've had to walk all
over Iceland on my head. What am I?
—*A horseshoe nail.* (ICELAND.)

> What is the shallow pool surrounded by a
> hedge?
> —*The eye (and eyelashes).* (JAVA.)

What lives in the water and is not a fish?
It wags two horns and is not a buffalo.

—*A snail.* (INDIA: BENGAL.)

> Who is the woodchopper who goes into the woods and cuts down a thousand trees at a single stroke?
>
> —*A barber.* (INDIA: KASHMIR.)

Who stands dumb until he is slapped—
and then he speaks out?

—*A drum.* (INDIA: SANTAL.)

> The brother always stays at home when his sister goes for a walk. Who are they?
>
> —*A lock and its key.* (INDIA: PARSEE.)

What is the biggest musical instrument in the world?

—*Thunder.* (INDIA: BHIL.)

> It has a red crest and is not a cock;
> It has a green back and is not a peacock;
> It has a long tail and it not a monkey;
> It has four legs and is not a horse.
> What is it?
>
> —*The common garden lizard.*
> (INDIA: BIHAR.)

What leaves the village in silence but makes a deafening sound when it reaches the jungle?

—*An ax.* (INDIA: HO.)

There was a man and no man,
He had a gun and no gun,
He shot a bird and no bird,
Upon a tree and no tree.
—*A boy with a popgun shot a butterfly on a hollyhock.* (IRELAND.)

What pulls without hands, runs without feet and bites without a mouth?
—*The wind.* (ITALY.)

There was a king who ruled no people—
He sailed a ship in the middle of the sea;
He sent a messenger without a letter
And got an answer that was not written.
—*Noah, the Ark, the dove and the olive branch.* (ISRAEL.)

How is a kite with a broken string like a boat without a rudder?
—*Nobody can tell where either will go.* (JAPAN.)

What is it that stands in the field with its hair disheveled?
—*Corn on a stalk.* (KOREA.)

A hundred-year-old man wears a hat that is only one day old. What is that?
—*A tree covered with snow.* (LAPLAND.)

My father went to war and killed a rooster, which crowed again at daybreak. What did he do?
—*He cut down a plantain tree, which sprouted up again before morning.* (LIBERIA.)

What is the room with occupants, that can
go through a window?
—*A fishnet, when pulled through a hole
in the ice.* (LITHUANIA.)

> An iron father and a wooden mother have
> many little bloodthirsty children. What is
> that?
> —*A gun barrel, the gunstock and bullets.*
> (LATVIA.)

What has a mouth to eat with but no
stomach to put the food into?
—*Scissors.* (MADAGASCAR.)

> What is it that is a snake and isn't a snake?
> —*A snake's sloughed-off skin.* (MALAYA.)

What is very black outside and very
white inside?
—*A pot full of rice.* (MAURITIUS.)

> I'm not a soldier, yet I fight;
> I never studied music, yet I sing;
> I'm not a clock, yet I call out certain
> hours.
> What am I?
> —*A rooster.* (MEXICO.)

The house is full of gray wool
And you can't catch a handful.
—*Smoke.* (NORWAY.)

> Who is the Sufi with an arrow through his
> middle who winds a turban round his waist
> and then whirls about the street?
> —*A spinning top.* (PERSIA.)

What is it that from head to foot is all tongue?
—*Fire.* (PERSIAN DERVISHES.)

> What are the ten stones that you always carry at your sides?
> —*Your fingernails.* (AZTECS OF ANCIENT MEXICO.)

What was born in the field and now dances round in the living room?
—*A broom.* (PERU.)

> How can you travel very fast yet never leave the place you start from?
> —*Swing in a hammock.*
> (PHILIPPINE REPUBLIC.)

Who is the little boy wearing a red cap who sits on a shelf by the stove?
—*A match.* (POLAND.)

> What is this: Five oxen and a stick are sowing black seeds over a white field?
> —*The fingers, a pen, ink and paper.*
> (PORTUGAL.)

What is the wonderful thing that we swallow, which can also swallow us?
—*Water.* (PUERTO RICO.)

> I have no tongue, yet I tell people their faults.
> They don't appear to get angry, for they always keep me around.
> What am I?
> —*A mirror.* (RUMANIA.)

Who are these: a fat mother, a red daughter and a grumbling son?
—*A stove, coals and the flame.*
(SIBERIA: YAKUT.)

> Snow is falling from a tiny sky—what is that?
> —*Flour falling from a sifter.*
> (ASIATIC RUSSIA: TATAR.)

What neither burns in fire nor drowns in water?
—*Ice.* (RUSSSIA.)

> What house is built with work done only by the mouth?
> —*A bird's nest.* (NORTHEASTERN RUSSIA: VOTYAK.)

Who are the seven brothers: six are slaves of the other one and have to search for his food?
—*The legs, arms and eyes all work for the mouth.* (SAMOA.)

> Through the woods and through the woods
> And through the woods I ran;
> And every bush that I cam till,
> I left my rags and ran.
> —*A sheep left its wool on every thorn.*
> (SCOTLAND.)

I am so small and so frightened of the Bogeyman that I always light my lamp at nightfall. What am I?
—*A firefly.* (SPAIN.)

What is nothing but holes tied to holes,
and yet is strong as steel?
—*A chain.* (SWEDEN.)

> What bird can pronounce his own name?
> —*The cuckoo.* (SWITZERLAND.)

What is it that is born twice but dies only
once?
—*A fowl; born first as an egg and second
when the egg hatches.* (TIBET.)

> A beautiful fairy sat on a green throne,
> but when I reached for her a rider drew
> a sword. What is that?
> —*A rose on a thorny bush.* (TURKEY.)

What can't work without having something
in its eye?
—*A needle.* (WALES.)

> A snake that God created wears a saddle
> made by man. What is it?
> —*A river with a bridge across it.* (SERBIA.)

What is silver outside and gold inside?
—*An egg.* (ARMENIA.)

> What is it that is neither far away nor near,
> and you can always just catch a glimpse
> of it?
> —*Your nose.* (THAILAND.)

What has hair outside and hair inside, yet
people stuff still more hair into it?
—*A fur cap.* (HUNGARIAN GYPSIES.)

I planted a board:
From the board grew a rope;
From the rope grew a bell;
From the bell grew a ball.
—*A pumpkin seed, the vine, the flower and the fruit.* (DOMINICAN REPUBLIC.)

    Fluffy sat down on Smoothy and swore not to rise until Smoothy became Fluffy. What is that?
    —*A setting hen and an egg.* (GUATEMALA.)

If you walk on the living ones they won't holler,
But if you walk on the dead ones they will holler.
—*Green leaves and dry leaves.*
(BARBADOS: BRITISH WEST INDIES.)

    Hard as a rock, not rock;
    White as milk, not milk;
    Sweet as sugar, not sugar.
    —*A coconut.*
    (GRENADA: BRITISH WEST INDIES.)

I had an egg that wouldn't break, even if I threw it six miles. What was it?
—*A ball.*
(ST. EUSTATIUS: BRITISH WEST INDIES.)

    My father has a house with the floor on top and the roof underneath. What is it?
    —*A boat.*
    (ST. MARTIN: BRITISH WEST INDIES.)

Four bottles of milk are uncorked and upside down, and not a drop leaks out. What is that?

—*A cow's udder.*
(MONTSERRAT: BRITISH WEST INDIES.)

My father has a cow: The cow stands still and the rope is running. What is it?

—*A pumpkin on a vine.*
(TRINIDAD: BRITISH WEST INDIES.)

A bullfrog jumps from bank to bank and his little feet never touch the ground. What is that?

—*A spider swinging.*
(BAHAMAS: BRITISH WEST INDIES.)

I have a hen with six chickens: When I hold the hen the chickens cry. What is that?

—*A six-stringed guitar.*
(JAMAICA: BRITISH WEST INDIES.)

Sampson's Riddle:

Out of the eater came forth food, and out of the strong came forth sweetness.

—*Sampson ate honeycomb made by bees in a lion's skeleton.* (THE OLD TESTAMENT.)

There is a place cut up by gullies. What is it?

—*An old woman's face.* (OMAHA INDIANS.)

It is grumbling. Beyond the mountain
smoke is rising; it chases away the cari-
bous. What is that?
—*A boiling kettle. Children, take care!*
(ESKIMO.)

        What do you eat to live?
        —*Buffalo meat.* (ARAPAHO INDIANS.)

What kind of noise makes you feel small?
—*Thunder.* (COMANCHE INDIANS.)

        What goes whistling along the cliffs?
        —*A bear's nose.*
        (DENE INDIANS OF ARCTIC CANADA.)

What went to the North Pole and stopped
there,
And came back because it couldn't go
there?
—*A watch.* (NEWFOUNDLAND.)

        Over the water, under the water,
        Round the world it ranges;
        Never been seen by the eye of man,
        But oftentimes it changes.
        —*The mind.* (NOVA SCOTIA.)

Who was born but never died?
—*You and many others.*
(PENNSYLVANIA GERMAN.)

        Who teaches without talking?
        —*A book.* (AFRICA: WOLOF.)

I have great powers and little strength:
I open closed houses and close open
ones; I guard the master's house and he
guards me.

—*A key.* (LATIN.)

>I tremble at each breath of air,
>And yet can heaviest burdens bear.
>
>—*Water.* (CANADA.)